The Book of Y

The Book of Y

Life, the Universe, and Elephant Dung

Peter Meadows and
Joseph Steinberg

Authentic

MILTON KEYNES ● COLORADO SPRINGS ● HYDERABAD

13 12 11 10 09 08 07   7 6 5 4 3 2 1

First published in 2007 by Authentic Media
9 Holdom Avenue, Bletchley, Milton Keynes, Bucks, MK1 1QR
1820 Jet Stream Drive, Colorado Springs, CO 80921, USA
OM Authentic Media, Medchal Road, Jeedimetla Village,
Secunderabad 500 055 A.P., India
www.authenticmedia.co.uk

Authentic Media is a division of IBS-STL U.K., limited by guarantee, with its Registered
Office at Kingstown Broadway, Carlisle, Cumbria CA3 OHA. Registered in England & Wales
No. 1216232. Registered charity 270162

British Library Cataloguing in Publication Data

A catalogue record for this book is available from
the British Library.

ISBN-13 978-1-86024-568-8

Cover design by Daniella Meyer
Print Management by Adare Carwin
Printed in Great Britain by J.H. Haynes and Co., Sparkford

Contents

FIRSTLY . . .

Have you noticed how few of the world's really important questions ever seem to get asked? For every zillion inquiries as to "Does my rear look big in this?" you'll hear hardly even one "Why was I made?" or "Is this all there is to life?"

Of course "Does my rear . . . ?" questions matter, especially if you give the wrong answer. But nothing can matter more than life's most important questions and that's the reason for *The Book of Y*.

It's a book for those who want to discover more than simply what their college friends are doing now. Or whether the Vulcan nerve pinch is only a myth. It's for those open to taking a serious look—without getting too anally retentive—at what matters above all else.

As you read, the voice you'll "hear" is mine (Peter's). But this has been a tag-team effort. The mighty snarling duo of Meadows and Steinberg has been at work. So ask "Who wrote that bit?" and the answer will come "We both did."

Not that *The Book of Y* has been our effort alone. Our thanks go to those who have played their part in influencing its content. And to a myriad of others—ancient and modern—who have had their thoughts and words plundered.

The Book of Y has its roots in an earlier book of ours. But though much of that book's structure has remained, much of its content hasn't. We couldn't deny you the tin squash ball, the plastic man and the windmill thing, or the bra straps and buckets.

Our goal has been to craft a down-to-earth book about the big questions of life for "ordinary" sane and sensible people. One that didn't call for brains to be parked, or a whole new vocabulary to be learned.

As your guides, we must own up to some firmly held conclusions—based on our own journey of inquiry made over the past thirty years or so.

Indeed, the terrain you are about to scramble over has become familiar to us. And we both have found it to have some wonderful "views." Views that, for us, have become personal convictions gradually and positively reshaping every aspect of our lives—in a way we would have once considered beyond belief.

Are we—and the more than one and a half billion, spread right across the globe, who share our convictions—simply deluded? Or is there, as we are convinced, genuinely more to life?

Please suspend your honest disbelief for a while and let's go find out. Step this way. And watch out for the elephant dung.

Peter and Joseph

LIFE SUCKS

Is there more to life than this?

Sometimes, let's be honest, life can be as much fun as stuffing marsh-mallows up your nose. Gargling with lemon juice. Or scratching your eyeballs with a fork.

I'm reminded of a hamster and its owner. Each morning Sam hits the wheel, stopping only to snatch a bite to eat, driven on by some ingrained belief that all the effort is getting him somewhere. Trudge, trudge, trudge. Nibble, nibble, nibble. With only occasional treats to break the monotony.

Poor old Sam. And for this thirty-something's pet hamster it is almost as bad!

Of course, life does have its great moments. We each spend enough money and energy making sure of that. The chase is on for bigger, faster, glossier, and newer. Toys for the girls as well as the boys. If only ageing could be delayed—and we could count on one day being an octo-genarian sex machine—then life would be perfect. If only the anti-ageing cream could prolong teenage looks forever—and didn't taste so bad.

Yet, when we have conquered all known lands, accumulated all the possessions there are to be had, strolled the world's finest beaches and finally figured out how to program the DVD recorder—what then? Suppose when we finally reach the top of the ladder it turns out to be leaning against the wrong wall?

Of course, some have life worse than others. Like the husband whose wife came home to find him in the kitchen, shaking frantically with what looked like a wire running from his waist toward the toaster. To jolt him away from the deadly electrical current she whacked him

1

with a plank of wood. Until that moment the man had been happily jiggling to his iPod. Now his arm was broken in two places.

Or spare a thought for someone called John Bloor—who mistook a tube of superglue for his hemorrhoid cream. Enough said.

Sound the drum too for the twenty-five-year-old poacher from the Russian town of Tula. To catch fish he put a live electrical cable into a pond. Sadly he didn't think to remove it before wading in to retrieve his spoils—meeting the same fate as the fish. If only he'd had his wife handy with a plank of wood—maybe he too would only have a broken arm.

Then there was Paul Stiller and his wife Bonnie—who landed in a New Jersey hospital. While driving around at 2 a.m., the bored couple lit a stick of dynamite to toss out of the car window just to see what would happen. Neither had thought to roll down the window.

All these were recipients of runner-up prizes in the *Darwin Awards*. This annual honor goes to those who provide the universal human gene pool the biggest service—by getting killed in the most extraordinarily stupid way. Or did something so crassly dumb that they really ought to be removed from the human gene pool.

But the list of unenviable lives does not end there. Think of the two robbers who tried to hold up a bus in Brazil while armed only with a hairdryer. Only to be shot by a passenger who had a real gun.

Though my favorite dumbster story of all, surely just an urban legend, is of Friedrich Riesfeldt. This unfortunate zookeeper, from Paderborn in Germany, set out to solve the problem of a seriously constipated elephant. His solution involved a potent cocktail of 22 doses of animal laxative and more than a bushel of berries, figs, and prunes. Not satisfied, the overzealous Friedrich then attempted to give the ailing elephant an olive-oil enema, at exactly the moment nature dramatically—and fatally—took its course.

The initial blast of pachyderm poop knocked the unwary zookeeper to the ground, striking his head on a rock. There he lay unconscious—as the animal continued to evacuate another 200 pounds of animal excrement from its bowels. It was at least an hour before a watchman came along. By which time poor Fred—though warm and comfortable—had suffocated.

Life may never get that bad for us, but we know what it is to live in a world of uncertainty and confusion. To plod through an existence of considerable pain but with little gain in real terms. Where "okay" is often as good as it gets. Where the thought of life having an overall purpose and lasting fulfillment seldom has time even to enter our over-busy minds.

But sooner or later, probably when some event of life stops us in our tracks, the haunting thought nags away—"Is this all there is?"

Powerless in an Uncertain World

For a start, far too much that matters seems to be totally outside our own control. The planet we live on and the way governments and other major players behave, and so much more, leaves us fearing both the present and the future.

The environment: Those who know keep telling us we are treating our world even worse than many treat their bodies. Selfishness, greed, and sheer stupidity are slowly turning a magnificent specimen into a wheezy out-of-condition mess. Yes, that's not me I'm talking about but our increasingly tarnished blue planet.

The reality of global warming brings a chill to the air as it melts ice caps and glaciers, threatening the future of whole coastal communities and those who depend on them. The forests we need to maintain an ecological balance are increasingly for the chop. Meanwhile, the world's chemical industries infest our environment with a torrent of toxic materials—threatening rivers and lakes, our air, land and oceans and ultimately ourselves and our future.

Internationally: Who would dare leave their lunchtime snack unattended in a public place? Once the worst that could happen was it would go missing and you'd go hungry. Now it could start a major security alert, with your BLT blasted into a million bacon bits. If only all the consequences of a world rampant with war, conflict and terrorism were that trivial.

From the beaches in Bali to the commuter trains in your neck of the woods, life is more at risk than ever. Worse still, there is no negotiating table for anyone to sit round. Just home-made videos that scream "death to the infidels"—who happen to be you and me.

Our own vulnerability: One of the key words sociologists are using to describe our society is "anxiety." It's easy to see why.

We feel increasingly less safe—with CCTV cameras and multiple locks on our doors all making the point. How long before the mandatory Christmas present is a body implant for children, offering global tracking?

My friend Joseph Steinberg has vivid memories of returning after only eight days away—to discover his home had been burgled at least three times. In fact, the thieves kept coming back for more. The police even found stuff stored by the back door ready for the next visit.

Joseph describes what he found as "like the Goldilocks story on crack." The beds were messed up. The couch was slashed. The office-study was trashed. Drawer contents were poured out. Hamburgers lay half-cooked on the grill. Beer cans and cigarette butts were strewn around. In a final ironic twist, one of the windows of his newly installed "protect-your-home-better" double glazing had been removed to let the looters in.

Soon, no doubt, we'll be able to respond to friends like this with a greeting card from the Bad News section. Cards with genuinely useful messages like "Sorry to Hear You Have Been Burgled," "Smile, It's Only a Mugging!" "Even the Best People Can Lose Everything" and "Best Wishes for the Swift Recovery of Your Car."

Anxiety doesn't stop there. Every email brings the threat of a virus that will destroy our hard drive and poison our pets. Or offer a scam to rob us of the contents of our savings or our personal identity.

Meanwhile, world events too often seem to be the proverbial flap of a butterfly's wing that causes a hurricane to derail our own plans, circumstances, and security.

A sick chicken in Asia takes us from where birds flew to one where they have the flu—deadly enough to potentially inflict death on hundreds of thousands. H5N1 is just one more risk, along with BSE, SARS and other yet-to-be announced initials that spell "A-N-X-I-E-T-Y."

And all the while we are anxious as to whether anyone is telling us the truth about any of it—and a lot more besides. After all, it is not only presidents that can look you in the eye while lying through their teeth or who simply can't be trusted. Global and respectable names like Andersen and Enron have proved that with panache.

Who can be confident they know the truth about anything? Did Diana have no more than an accident? Were there weapons of mass destruction? Are hamburgers safe to eat? Did the Pentagon hurl itself in the path of a passenger jet? Was Area 51 for real? Did the old woman really live in a shoe?

We simply don't know who, what, why, where or when any more.

Disposable Relationships

Being subject to the whims of world events is one thing. But it keeps raining right on our own personal parade too. "Till death us do part" becomes "Until I get bored or receive a better offer." The land of marriage is full of temporary residents; those "just passing through." As a result, we now have a society where relationships have become almost as disposable as razor blades. Once used, we're just tossed in the trash. That hurts.

Swing while you are winning is turning great swathes of the population into losers. The scars of broken relationships—even when there is no obvious betrayal—are not always on the outside. Break apart two bricks that have been cemented together and notice how each leaves parts of itself behind with the other. That's exactly how many of us can feel. Less complete. Less fulfilled. Undervalued, used, abused, and cast aside.

Pressured Lives

Whatever our role in life, the demand is that we do more with less. But at least there are some great words to make it seem normal— "Downsizing," "Rationalization," "Economy of scale," "Market forces."

Meanwhile, our information "rich" society bombards us with an ever-increasing deluge of spam. Messages we don't want or need are mingled with the constant barrage of phone calls, email, faxes, Internet bulletins, texts, and even the occasional letter.

And whether you are a none, one- or two-income household, the pressure is relentlessly on to keep up. Keep up with the fashion, the gizmos, the pace, the party, the "latest," the whatever. Just keep up keeping up.

Ever wonder what those laboratory rats feel like while trying to work from one end of the maze to the other just to earn that little piece of cheese? How much different is that to what we so often call "life"?

On the domestic front it's no less stressful. With so much going on, you fear the moment you'll take your child to the vet, the dog to the dentist, make coffee with the gravy mix, fix your hair with furniture polish. And the dinner ends up on the ceiling.

Feeling powerless yet? "No," you reply, "I was feeling powerless before you started all this. Now I feel like a snowman in a deep fat fryer." Well, join the meltdown club. Never have so many people felt such a fear about their future or a lack of satisfaction with the here and now.

So where are you on the board game of life? Each day you roll the dice and move on. From driving license to job, to a place of your own, to a partner, to kids, to their education, to retirement, to decay, to . . .? And when we finally "win," then what? None of the trinkets we have accumulated can go with us. What's it all about?

A Bigger Picture?

Life seems beyond belief sometimes, doesn't it? Totally outside our control or ability to understand. So we keep our heads down and keep moving. Like Sam and his hamster.

But supposing—just supposing—there was a bigger picture. One that made sense of all we think we know already. One that could help us fulfill our deepest longings.

Perhaps you've seen that classic painting of the chubby angelic cherub, with plump face resting on even plumper hands. Wings spread while eyes reach heavenwards in adoration. The face has become an icon—on greetings cards, place mats, framed pictures. And I'm entranced by it.

What a shock when I came across a print with not only this familiar heavenly being but a "twin" alongside it. What a revelation to discover this cherub was part of a bigger picture. One I had never realized existed. And there was more.

This famous cherub—deservedly admired in its own right far and wide—makes up only a fraction of a magnificent painting by Raphael. Of course, I had been fully satisfied with the pleasure the little cherub gave me. But now I saw it was only a small detail of a larger work. Here was a whole world to be explored and enjoyed that was beyond my wildest dreams.

Could this be an expression of how life is? Could there be more outside the frame, a bigger picture you've never seen? Is it possible the "God" you call on when things go wrong might really exist? And could this even be the key to making sense of everything else?

So, now we've hyperventilated together, take a minute or two for a deep breath, a soothing cup of chai or, better yet, a Häagen-Dazs. And prepare to roll back the curtains and look at some clues that this isn't all there is.

DESIGNS ON YOU

Are there any clues to the "God" question?

Can it really be, in the great scheme of things, each of us is no more significant than a boil on the backside of a baboon? When all is said and done, is that all there is?

When our clogs have been popped, our bucket kicked, and the daisies well and truly pushed up, have we done no more than make a microscopic contribution to the human gene pool? And have we been of no more consequence than what was once a squirrel but is now only a faint blur in the middle of the road?

If there is no God then the answer in every case has to be "yes." But there is a vast amount of evidence to suggest a very different story.

The Miracle of Life

Imagine this. There you were enjoying a pampered existence in a safe and secure home—where life was constantly like those sleepy moments between dusk and dawn. The sounds reaching your little ears were always at a muffled minimum. Feeding was effortless and just an umbilical cord away.

Life was such bliss as you floated around in a human cargo carrier. Then it happened—the big squeeze. An earthquake turned inside out. Moving lower all the time, you felt like toothpaste in the tube from hell. The push and shove from womb to world seemed an eternity. Then suddenly—mayhem. It was all bright lights, cold air—and some crazy person swinging you upside down and slapping your backside.

8

But that was not your only welcome. Somewhere there was a parent or two—reduced to jelly, their emotions a wreck. The sight of your slimy little wrinkled body had induced an intoxicating cocktail of joy, gratitude, and wonder that simply engulfed them.

Such is the miracle of life. An experience that dramatically focuses our attention on something or someone greater than ourselves.

At least that's how it's been for me—five times. Maybe you've never witnessed a birth and can't quite remember your own. But indulge me for a moment, because I think what happens in the delivery room provides a large clue toward answering the God question.

The fact of life

What is it that can so capture our attention? First there is the sheer miracle of life itself.

I will never forget the birth of our first son. Not because a stray blackbird flew in and began swooping round the delivery room. Or because of the initial panic when his first breath took so long to happen. But because I knew, overwhelmingly, that he represented something way beyond the united contribution of my wife and me.

It's funny really. We were so proud of our little bundle of joy but when it boils right down to it, no one can create life itself. We can map the human genome, but we cannot produce it. We can mangle and mess up organs and we can grow them again for transplant—but not from scratch. Ultimately, life begins somewhere beyond our power to create or recreate it.

So, at the birth of our son, I stood there wearing a stupid surgical cap, holding a little miracle in my hands while the tears ran down my cheeks. It was a "God moment," and I was so grateful I had someone bigger than myself to thank.

Above all else, it was the creation of life itself that was so astounding. My new child was far more than the sum total of his DNA or the combined value of his chemical compounds. That's why to lose a child is not an event in the same order as losing a rollover lottery ticket. That's why we spend billions of dollars in the aftermath of earthquakes and tsunamis. We humans claw our way through the rubble and remains of what used to be home because we really do matter to one another.

So, if the worst happens, and we lose our baby—that loss has nothing at all to do with the thought of wasting nine months of discomfort. Or "having to go through all that again." We treasure that new life because of what it represents if it stays—and what we lose if it goes.

Attention to detail

The second thing that captures our attention is the splendor of the packaging in which a new life is wrapped.

Eyes, hearing, reflexes, a motor mechanism that grips on an offered finger, a pre-programed understanding of what food is and how to find it. The tiny heart that patters away. And those little lungs so capable, from the first moments after birth, of breathing air—and then hurling it past vocal chords to create a sound more akin to an air raid siren than to the burbles of an innocent newborn.

This bundle is mind-blowingly complex—made up of 60 trillion cells, with each cell carrying more information than could be stored on the shelves of a university library. And it is also stunningly unique—with a never to be repeated blend of 6,000,000,000 distinct, separate and precise instructions that make up its genetic code.

To underscore the point, I was tempted to unpack for you the astounding complexity of just one organ—the eye. But I took pity on you. The simplest description I could find as to how light becomes sight ran to 623 closely typed and complex words. And it was festooned with everyday jargon like transducinrhodopsin and phosphodiesterase.

But the heart of the message was clear. The eye alone is so complex a mechanism—involving intricate chemical actions and minutely timed and accurate reactions—that the concept of it being no more than an accident stretches belief.

Not that new parents tend to be obsessed with physiological details when caught up in the wonder of the moment. Their comments are more likely to be limited to "oohs," "ahs," and "just look at those dinky little fingers." But the message is the same. Such a miracle of design and perfection turns our hearts and minds—however briefly—to the Someone who made it all possible.

A World of Design

The created wonder of that newborn child is but a speck in an equally complex universe. If the new parent takes a moment to look past their reflection in the window, to the night sky outside, their sense of awe can only increase.

This is another clue that there's somebody out there. Just like that tiny baby's body, so our planet and our solar system, our galaxy, even beyond to the universe—all of it—is infused not with randomness but with intricate and finely balanced design, all of which fits together like the pieces of a finely crafted clock.

Try this for size—

- If the ratio of protons to neutrons in creation were to change by more than one part in only 100,000,000,000,000,000,000,000,000,000,000,000,000—galaxiesand stars would not hold together.
- If the force of electromagnetism were slightly stronger or weaker, atoms would not be able to hold electrons properly and the necessary molecules for life would not exist.
- If there were the slightest variation in the velocity of light up or down, life would be impossible in the universe. We wouldn't be here and nor would anyone else.

Does that all strike you as something a little more than a piece of good luck? Random chance?

Instead of numbers, let me try you with a "picture." The first computer I ever bought came with a remarkable little program called "Orbits." It traces the complex and consistent relationship between the orbits of the planets in our solar system.

All I do is click on any two planets on the list provided and hit "go." One may expect the resulting picture to look like a bowl stuffed full of spaghetti. But within seconds a stunningly beautiful pattern—based on the constantly changing gravitational pull between the two planets—fills the screen. The effect is much like the Spirograph drawings of a past generation. Or a highly complex piece of lace filigree.

In this way it expresses the finely tuned design and balance of our universe. If either the shape of the orbits or the speed at which the planets travel are changed by as little as 1/1,000th the end result would be not a beautiful pattern, but a screen filled with something that looks more akin to the leftovers from last night's dinner.

All this design points to one obvious conclusion—a designer.

It makes sense. The marvelously created Taj Mahal didn't just appear on an Indian landscape one day. It gained the benefit of having gifted designers, builders, and zoning planners. They made sure it ended up in the right place, reflecting the abilities and aspirations of all those involved.

This is equally true of the lovely BMW K1200 R motorcycle. The awesome design both in body and engine—one that produces an amazing 160 bhp of torque on two wheels—had a whole team of technicians and designers behind it.

In other words, it is unthinkable to have design without a designer.

The Existence of Our Emotions

It is not only the things we can see and touch that point us to the likelihood of there being a Creator. The same is true of our feelings.

So how are you feeling? Happy? Sad? Hopeful? Angry? Do you appreciate beauty? Do you react against injustice or the exploitation of others? Our ability to feel such emotions is a further clue to there being more to life than this.

Think it through. If we are nothing more than the result of endless random mutations—with the survivors being those best equipped to do so— where do our emotions or conscience come from? They are not essential for our survival. In fact, feelings of pity for others put our personal future at risk—as they can lead to acts of self-sacrifice. Even children instinctually risk their lives to save an animal in distress or in danger of death. Where does that come from?

It has been suggested that our inbuilt sense of justice and fair play has nothing to do with a God who created us—that it comes from our social conditioning. The thinking is that everyone around us accepts these things and we have subconsciously bought into them also.

But if this is true, where did these concepts come from in the first place? How did a sufficient number of people initially hold to them strongly enough for us to be conditioned so well? And once again, how come children are obsessed with "it's not fair" long before they encounter the "rules" of grown-up society?

Our Sense That There is a God

Anthropologists know it. Archaeologists know it. From the very beginning of human history people have always and intrinsically believed in a Supreme Being. When ancient burial sites are excavated—along with the spear, bronze arrow, or golf club—there is usually some sort of idol or object which points to the deceased having believed in some sort of overarching deity or God.

We just can't help it. It is part of the very stuff we are made of—this deep, natural subconscious belief in a power or person bigger and greater than us.

During the starkly atheistic days of the former Soviet Union there were those who came to believe there must be a God on the basis that the authorities were so concerned to tell them there wasn't one. Their logic was simple: if there is no God there would be no need to tell us.

How wise they were. There has never been a campaign to deny the existence of the tooth fairy, or Santa—we know they are not real. And there has never been a time when the prevailing view of society was that there is no God—which is a huge pointer to the probability that there is one.

Even the very fact our reflexes lead us to call out to God in times of need—or shout abuse at him in times of disaster—points to the likelihood of his very existence.

What Could This God be Like?

So far we have noted the fact we are here, but not of our own making (well, not *exactly*). We are made up of minute detail and live within the context of a universe of intricate design. We have thought about the existence of our emotions and the innate sense most of us have that there is something or someone who exists beyond our five senses. But what could this God be like?

Before we go any further, I'd like permission to briefly blow your mind. Let's step back—way back—and consider some thoughts on the greatness of God.

We humans assume God is just like us only somewhat bigger—and older. We imagine his mind is much like ours—as are his feelings and actions. But that can't possibly be true. God can't be like us. He simply has to be far greater in every way—and wholly different from us. Let me explain.

God is bigger than space

Simple logic tells us design requires a designer, matter requires a maker, and motion requires an initiator. Therefore, in the beginning there could have been nothing but God—and then he rolled up his celestial sleeves and got to work. Interestingly, this is exactly the way the well-known opening of the Bible tells it, "In the beginning God created the heavens and the earth."[1]

What could that mean? Please lend me your imagination for a moment.

Imagine this very page you are looking at represents the universe—and the God who made it is there too. All the letters on the page are the stars and planets. So where do you picture God? Somewhere, mixed in the middle of the universe with all these letters perhaps? Maybe he's hiding behind the planet Pluto? But that cannot be.

Before God created, he was all there was—and I mean "ALL." So the only place God could put what he made was inside himself.

So let's start again. Now, imagine this page as blank—before any words were placed on it. In the beginning there was only God—he is the page. Then he created. Where did he put his handiwork? Here, on the page, *within* himself.

You see, in the beginning God had to create a space—a place to locate the universe. The only place he could put stars, planets, and all he created was inside of himself.

Even in the best conditions the human eye can see about 5,000 stars. But modern telescopes reveal a truly astronomical story: The number is 70 sextillion, or seven followed by 22 zeroes. Which, put simply, is more than the total number of grains of sand in all the Earth's beaches and deserts.

Which means, no matter how vast and immeasurable the cosmos may be, God can only be even greater.

God is greater than time

Before God began to create there was nothing—not even time itself. There was no such thing as time. No days, hours, minutes, seconds, and so on. Instead of "time" there was "eternity."

What do I mean by eternity? Most people think of eternity, or "for ever," as a lot of long chunks of time joined together. Not so. Time has limits and boundaries, starts and finishes, beginnings and endings, just like the bone in your forearm. Time, like everything else, has been created.

But eternity is of a different dimension. It is more like "super putty" or "flubber"—stretchy and expanding. Eternity has no beginning and no end. Just like a page that has no edges—it keeps on going and going with everything God created laid on top of it.

In a certain sense we can say that we have always lived in the context of time. But God has always lived in the context of eternity—a place which has no borders or boundaries, no margins or restrictions. Time, with its limitations, is the place where we currently live. Eternity, with its never-ending horizon, is the place where God lives and invites us to spend our for ever.

So let's go back to the page again and the use of your imagination. If God is this page and the letters and words represent his creation, how can you illustrate "time"? The answer is to draw a line, with a starting point and ending point, on the page. That would be time. And God will still be greater than the print contained on the page and the line drawn across it.

Scientists tell us the universe is 10 billion years old, others say 20 billion, some are still counting. With light traveling at 186,000 miles a second it is going to take billions of years to see all the mega-trillions of stars and millions of galaxies that are out there.

And the God who made it all is bigger than the lot of it. Bigger and utterly greater and different from everything he has created—even time itself.

God is interested in the smallest detail

As we begin to understand the vastness of God and his sheer size, compared to us, it would be easy to despair. "If God is so big," you may be thinking, "then certainly he has more important things on his mind than me."

But God is not only vast, he is also detailed. He can not only be seen and known in the grand magnitude of the universe, but also in the micro scale of the atom. And even in "little old you."

The utter complexity of design and individuality even in the smallest details of our world suggests God's interest. To know that every snowflake in a blizzard is uniquely different—every fingerprint in a crowd of twelve million commuters is exclusively distinct—these little marvels of constitution demonstrate the interest of the Creator.

Remember that baby we started out with? Such intricate design. Remember all those DNA particles—the chromosomes and cells, the atoms and all those little bits and pieces? They are like tiny little universes in their own right.

One of my highlights at Disney World, besides being mistaken for Goofy, was a ride at the Epcot Center where we were miniaturized and "injected" into the human body. It was an amazing adventure, where we were attacked by white blood cells, sucked through the chambers of the heart, breathed past tiny fibers in the lungs, and then the ultimate—we were electrocuted by tiny electron charges in the brain's neurones and shot back out into "our own world" again.

Just like the tiny ball of fluff that is another whole world, protected by Horton the elephant in Dr. Suess's *Horton Hears a Who!*, how many different alternative universes are there all around us that we never even notice?

But do you think the ant or the amoeba escapes God's eye? Not if he made them. He understands vertebrates, invertebrates, and even little blind fish down at the very bottom of the ocean. If *Honey, I Shrunk the Kids* were possible and we fell through the soil into some alien-looking termite hole, God would even be there too. If God made it in such incredible detail, how can he not care about it?

God is not only God of the macrocosm. For him to be God he must also be God of the microcosm. He cares about the universe as it is, set within himself, both large and small—even little ol' you.

A God Who Will Never Exhaust Our Exploration

Have you seen those Hubble space pictures? Stars, supernovas, and galaxy upon galaxy—swirling around so far away our minds cannot grasp what we are really seeing. There is a universe where no human has gone before—but desperately longs to do so. We are interested in seeing it, experiencing it, traveling through it, and—ultimately—in inhabiting it. Why? Because we have an insatiable desire to discover and experience more of all that surrounds us.

Imagine what it would be like if you knew everything there is to know. Nothing else at all was left to learn, discover or experience. How boring, frustrating, and pointless life would feel. If you knew it all, you would probably want to kill yourself out of sheer boredom. Then again, being a know-it-all would make it well nigh impossible to be able to choose from the countless methods available—better just to make everybody around you utterly miserable with your infinite intelligence.

But scientists tell us the universe is not static and limited, but ever-expanding—at an incredible rate. There will always be more for us to learn and experience. And yet still It Is easily contained within an "eternal" God.

The mind-stretching thing is this—if it is possible to know this eternally big God it would still take for ever to do so. And that's not bad news—it's good news. Imagine, always finding something new, always discovering just that little bit more. And I don't mean book knowledge. What I mean is more like falling in love over and over and over again— except with the same special person. So what we feel and experience always goes deeper and deeper. That Is what getting to know God, the one who made you, could be like.

Interested In You

So why did God do it? Why did he create it all—large and small? Was he somewhat bored as he hung about in eternity—and just fancied some exercise? Or is there a greater plan—one in which the human race is center stage?

There is an astounding contrast between humans and any other living species. Only human beings have expressed any desire or ability to reach out to a Creator. This means there is something unique about the relationship between God and us.

A human parent knows how they feel about the offspring from their loins. But how does the Creator God feel about us, as we who sprang from his? Or, more particularly, how does he feel about you?

Does he have the same desire for closeness and friendship that a parent harbors for their child? Why not? A child that lacks a deep "hugged by a loving embrace" relationship with a parent is missing their due. And—until we know God in the same way—could that be true of us?

If so, our whole life misses its meaning unless we relate to this eternal God in the way he desires.

If there is a God like this, nothing could be more important than knowing who he is, what he is like and what interest—if any—he has for us. To fail to do so would be like the man who lived by candle-power while scraping the mud off his shoes each night on what he thought was scrap iron. If only he had known this "useless junk" was a powerful generator, he could have had all the light and heat he ever dreamed of.

It would be like the man who took back his chainsaw after a week protesting that it did not do what the maker claimed.

"A tree every ten minutes was the promise," he complained. "The first day I only managed two. The next day I tried harder and managed four. Yesterday I pushed it to five. But I'm not happy."

Timidly the sales assistant ventured the question, "Could there be something wrong with the motor?"

"Motor? What motor?" the man replied. "You mean there's a switch to give it power?"

I hope I have switched you on. Because if God is there, creating a living relationship with him must be as important as breathing itself.

SECRET SPIDERS

Who knows enough to say for certain?

Despite all the clues to something or someone bigger than us, perhaps you still have honest doubts. You have heard the talk of design, purpose, inner conviction, and the rest, but wonder if such belief is but wishful thinking or childish delusion.

Your vote may remain with those who simply can't bring themselves to believe in a higher or greater power. With them you say something like, "As humankind grows to maturity it needs to shed such an outmoded belief—in much the same way as we no longer have any practical use for our appendix, washboards, and typewriters."

Let's imagine this is the way you see things. You are an atheist—a word taken from the Greek and which roughly translates as "no God." In which case, please help me for a moment by answering a simple question. Out of all the vast knowledge existing in the universe, how much of it do you personally possess? In other words, how much do you reckon you know of all that can be known?

Five percent? One percent? 0.0001 percent? The merest smidgen?

Now here's the rub—and a final question. Is it remotely possible for God to exist somewhere in that vast area of knowledge that is not yet yours?

To put it another way, is there a spider in your room? At this moment, I assume you can't see one, hear one, or smell one. But who would be so bold as to say with absolute certainty "This room is sans-spider"? Because somewhere, outside of your knowledge there may be a whole convention of them, just waiting to head for the shower.

To use examples from real life, who could believe in the existence of a stone that floats on water? But such a stone does exist. And who would countenance the existence of an animal with webbed feet and a bill that lays eggs like a duck but has fur and suckles its young? But such a creature is truly alive and well.

In the same way could, just possibly, God exist beyond your present comprehension, understanding, knowledge, and experience? Wouldn't someone with a half-open mind admit that it was at least a possibility?

But take care. Because to say "yes" means you are no longer an atheist but an agnostic—a small but significant step forward.

The word "agnostic" comes from the Greek word for knowledge and simply means "not knowing." It's a very honorable word, even though it's rather gone out of fashion—much like spiffing, snuff, and the Smurfs.

It's highly respectable to own up to not knowing whether there is or isn't a God. But only if you're the right kind of agnostic—because there are two very different sorts. There are "ornery" agnostics and "ordinary" agnostics.

The ornery agnostic says, "Not only do I not know if there is a God, neither do you or anyone. And nor will you know, now or for ever and ever"—making sure there is no "Amen" slipped in at the end.

In contrast, the ordinary agnostic says, "I don't know—but I'm open to knowing, should the right information come my way."

If you're the ornery, then goodbye and goodnight. There is nowhere for us to go from here. Your mind's set, closed, and that's that. But, if you're the ordinary, the following pages represent the most incredible journey you can imagine. But first we have to face an overwhelming problem.

The Problem of Discovering What God Is Like

So here you are, impressed by the clues and open-minded enough to dig a little further. You're ready to find answers to the big question, "What exactly could this God be like?" And it's at this point you hit the buffers—because there is no way you or anyone else—left to their own devices—can find out.

We may be able to establish some general principles but to take things any further than that is beyond us. Does that come as a shock? I'll do my best to explain.

Think through some of the key questions that need answers so far as the God agenda is concerned.

- Are we talking about a force or a personality? He, she or it?
- If this God is/has a personality, what values and feelings does "he" have—indifference, kindness, goodness, revenge? Or what?
- What are "his" plans, purposes, and expectations of the planet and its people—including us personally?
- Does "he" have mood swings?
- Is "he" one of many—or one without equal?
- Does "he" take it out on people who don't toe the line—or turn a blind eye?
- Has this God, having set everything in motion, retreated to a safe distance to watch how it all turns out—like pre-programing a washing machine?
- Or does God involve "himself" in the day-by-day moment-by-moment affairs of all that has been created?

These are big questions. The temptation is to believe that all it will take is a little logic and some stirring of the gray matter for the answers to pop into place. Please think again—because there are some solid reasons why trying to use our own mental capacity to crack the God code will land us in the theological soup. These same reasons also help explain why so many people have such varied ideas as to what God is like.

There Is a Limit to Our Knowledge

First, we don't have enough knowledge at our disposal. Face it—we have yet to find a cure for the common cold. So how can we possibly believe we know enough to discover the answers to the huge God-shaped questions?

If you have never tasted pawpaw, how can you describe the taste? If you have never heard *Wind Beneath My Wings* played backwards on a kazoo, how can you explain the sound?

Without a PhD in microbiology, how can you tell me what it is my aunt baked me for my birthday? Or, if you don't have a degree in computer engineering, how can you tell me why my Windows PC does the frustrating things it does, while my Mac just works?

The problem of the limit of human knowledge is perfectly displayed in the person of Christopher Columbus, who "discovered" America. The reason the Native Americans were called Red Indians is down to him. Sploshing ashore on the beach, dear old Chris was utterly convinced he'd arrived in India. The natives were probably too polite to tell him he was a tad out in his calculations. This is no big deal if you're only out searching for continents. But when checking out the Deity, a lack of the information you need becomes a more serious matter.

The story is told of six blind men given the task of describing an elephant—an animal outside the previous experience of them all.

Said the first, feeling its tail, "It's like a rope."
Said the second, feeling its body, "No, it's like a wall."
Said the third, feeling its trunk, "No, it's like a snake."
Said the fourth, feeling a leg, "No, it's like a tree."
Said the fifth, grabbing a tusk, "It's like a spear."
Said the sixth, taking hold of an ear, "It's like a fan."

The problem we all face, like those six blind men, is the God we are inquiring about is vastly bigger than our sphere of knowledge. He is therefore beyond our ability to discover what he is really like, except in a gropingly inadequate blind-man-meets-elephant way.

There Is a Limit to Our Reasoning Power

It's not just our knowledge that falls short but also our ability to reason.

A child asks "Why?" and "How?" and "Why?" again. And again. The parent has the answers and would love to be able to give them. But the child's intellectual ability does not stretch far enough—to say the least.

That's how it is when exploring the God agenda. Our brainpower does not match the task.

It's like trying to compete in a NASCAR race on roller skates. Or trying to illuminate an airport runway with birthday candles. It's like asking the average six-year-old to grasp the intricacies of algebraic trigonometry. Only worse.

In terms of our ability to wrap our minds round all that God entails, we are as sharp as marbles. Indeed, we have about as much to offer as the woman in an American town in Arkansas who had been in her parked car, with her hands clasped behind her head, for over two hours. At the beginning she had appeared to be asleep but finally her eyes were open and she looked somewhat strange.

Help was at hand when a concerned observer knocked on the glass to ask, "Are you okay?"

The woman answered, "I've been shot in the head, and I am holding my brains in."

The paramedics came rushing, to make the surprising discovery that the woman was fit and well—but had thick white stuff on the back of her head and in her hands. Investigation revealed the full story.

It was the middle of summer and the intense heat in the car had caused a canister of ready-to-cook bread dough to explode. And, with the noise of a gunshot, the contents hit her in the head. The woman had reached back to investigate. On feeling the dough, she became convinced it was her brains. And passed out from fright while attempting to hold them in!

We may hold human intellect in high esteem—or to the back of our heads with our hands. But we are simply not able to comprehend a God of such vastness and complexity through the use of human reason alone.

A God who can fit neatly within the scope of our limited understanding is bound to be a distortion of what is true and real.

There Is a Bias to Our Judgment

My friend, Joseph Steinberg, recently went to the dentist with an awful pain in his back tooth. He was hoping against hope there was nothing wrong—even though it felt like potential disaster was lurking somewhere beneath the enamel.

His choice was to have the tooth filled, being determined to believe the pain was not as real as it felt. Unfortunately, despite his hopes—and my "Love to your gums from all your chums" card—the pain got much worse. He began eating softer and softer foods so he could convince himself there was no real problem.

It was just three days later when, slowly and carefully chewing his over-boiled rice dinner, he heard a loud "CRACK!" As white light and shards of pain filled his vision, he elegantly spat out his food and half a back tooth. It had been fractured all along—right down the middle.

What Joseph had been after was short-term gain rather than the long-term truth—and he lost a tooth in the process. And when we go looking for the reality of what God is like we face the same problem. We would prefer to find only the things that would please us. We would rather only have information that adds to our comfort.

Our own self-interest drives us to limit our discoveries about God to those things that fit our comfort zones, mesh with our timetables, and accommodate our priorities. But God may well not be like that at all.

After all, suppose what we found revealed something unpalatable about ourselves or unwelcome about God? We would have no motivation to dig it out, even if our limited knowledge made it possible to do so.

In other words, our "search" for God is going to be like the assessment of a house-seller describing their property—rather than the verdict of the prospective purchaser's surveyor. Consciously or subconsciously, we are interested in focusing on what we want to find to be true rather than what may actually be the state of play.

The Only Answer—Is For God to Open the Communication

So is there no hope? Are we doomed to never know what is true and real about this God for whom there are such compelling clues? Can we only contribute our own speculation to that of every other voice—and so add to the confusion?

Not at all. But if there is to be a solution to our problem it has to come through the initiative of this God himself. Let me illustrate what I mean.

Jaws 3 was a goldfish our family won at the fair. We loved him (or her). We were never sure if the little thing understood where the daily supply of flakes came from or how much simple pleasure he gave us.

There was also no way Jawsie could comprehend our world, how we thought of him, or the extent we wished him to stop intimidating Bruno—his black guppy bowl-mate.

The only way to put that right, had it been possible, was for one of us to actually become a goldfish, enter the planktonized world of our fishy friend, and talk his language on his territory. There was just no other way he could get the message as to who we were, what we were like, and what our hopes for him were.

In the same way, if there's to be any possibility of us discovering the vastness and wonder of God, there is only one way it can happen. This is by God taking the initiative to make himself known to us. Our only hope is for this great big God, bigger than time and space, bigger than the universe itself, to somehow enter our world. For him to become like one of us, speak our language, see life through our eyes, suffer as we suffer and to give us a visible demonstration of what is true and real about him.

Of course, the thought that God could show up in our world flies in the face of all human logic—as I realized during a remarkable holiday encounter.

With two companions I had waited patiently for a seat in an overcrowded rooftop restaurant in a small Portuguese village. It was one of those nights when everyone had swarmed out to enjoy a perfect summer evening. The waiter's invitation came: "You wait an hour or share with one nice man who is nearly finished."

And so we found ourselves sharing a meal with Mr. MENSA—Brains of the Universe. Our new companion—already significantly lubricated with the house red—turned out to be the Dean of a major American university. To say he had brainpower is an understatement—fluency in four languages and several graduate degrees all sheltered beneath his high-domed and suntanned brow.

Our group sat mesmerized as our new friend, Dan, escorted us on a tour of his vast knowledge of human thought and wisdom so far as God and all things deistic were concerned. And then came the moment when it went threateningly quiet—as he condescended to ask what I believed and how it fitted into the picture.

Time froze. It felt like the recurring dream of being caught in the supermarket in only an under-length T-shirt. "Me?" I quavered—wondering how foolish I was about to sound.

But then I heard my mouth saying . . . "Everything you've said sounds like humankind looking for God. But I believe God came searching for us." And I metaphorically tugged the T-shirt a little lower, while waiting for the anticipated verbal pat on the head from an academic 20 years my senior. It didn't come.

"Wow. That's absolutely fantastic. I've never heard anything like it before. So deep," came the explosive and unexpected response.

Thus began an intriguing friendship, in which Dan afforded me the status of genius. Together the four of us explored the coast, while I helped this massive intellect understand that even a turbo-brain with twin exhausts and an overhead camshaft is not up to figuring out God for himself.

God Came Into Our World

But isn't it beyond belief to even dream that the Creator of the whole shebang would come looking for us? Nevertheless, this is exactly what has happened.

At a given point in human history God left the timelessness of eternity and vastness of the universe and beyond to enter our world. He was raised as any other child would have been raised in Israel some 2,000 years ago. But this "man-who-was-God" lived a life so significantly different; one with such a unique significance that history still shakes from its impact.

That man, of course, was Jesus. Of the fact that he lived there can be no doubt. There is too much evidence from the historians of his day to reach any other conclusion. I am thinking of writers like Tacitus, Suetonius, and Pliny, and the most well known of them all, Josephus, a Jewish historian who lived in Rome and died about AD 100.

Not all those who recorded Jesus' existence were his followers or agreed with what he did or said. But they did all accept that he lived. Indeed, although Josephus speaks dismissively of Jesus as "the so-called Messiah," he records his life, his death by crucifixion and that "on the third day he appeared to them restored to life."

The fact that Jesus lived is a matter of record. The rest, as they say, is history.

God Spoke Our Language

In Jesus, God took the initiative to make the details of his character and intentions of his heart known to those he had created. To do this

- He was born to ordinary working people in a humble town in an insignificant Mediterranean country.
- He identified in every way with those he had created—even down to being born as a racial minority, experiencing life as a refugee, and living in an occupied land.
- He passed up any special treatment for himself in the way of palace or privilege and so truly became one of us.
- He felt pain, hunger, tiredness, disappointment, and betrayal.
- He took up the cause of the outcast and lonely, the misunderstood and underprivileged while being misunderstood himself.

Of course, it's some claim to assert that this Jesus was actually God. Couldn't we settle for him being just a supercharged version of Gandhi, Mother Teresa, Bono, and David Blaine all rolled into one—a kind of humanitarian, wise, wonder-working magician?

We are about to face that very question.

WHO'S WHO?

Just another Gandhi or Mother Teresa?

Whatever you may think about Jesus, you have to admit there's something very strange about him. Not least, "How did such a small pebble make such a huge wave?" And by "huge" I mean HUGE.

Historians often sing out of tune with each other. But on one issue they all hit the same note. It's that Jesus affected history more than any other person to have breathed air on planet Earth.

Think of it. The best even the most influential world-changers can claim is to have roads, buildings, or even great cities named after them. But here is someone who even has the calendar dated from his birth. That's not a wave, it's a tsunami.

And though that decision was made in the ancient past, nothing has changed regarding the impact Jesus has made. Two thousand years after his birth, Google the name "Jesus" and you'll find well over 222 million pages referring to him. Okay, a few are about Spanish plumbers or Mexican *mariachi* guitarists with very religious mothers. But the rest demonstrates the unequalled level of interest, intrigue, and dedication surrounding the person of Jesus.

Of course you'll be wondering how Jesus' Googlocity rating matches up with other big history makers. Are 222 million pages outstanding? I wondered too—and checked to find out. The king—Elvis—was way out in front of the rest with a mere 81 million. Mohammed came next with 46 million pages. Next was Buddha with just over 39 million and Ghandi trailed last with just under 4 million. In other words, there's Jesus and there's the rest.

World-Changer from the Backwoods?

Yet—and here we come back to there being something "strange" about Jesus—has there ever been a less promising candidate? Be honest. If you were seeking a potential world-changer, would you go hunting among the population of an obscure backwoods town in a small enemy-occupied Mediterranean country?

Would you hand pick someone lacking much more than a basic education? Who never wrote a book or mixed with the rich and influential? Who, apart from a brief time as an infant refugee, never traveled more than 60 miles from his birthplace?

Someone who never did a stadium tour, hired a PR agent, or used a spin doctor? Didn't even have an extreme makeover?

Yet this so overwhelmingly unpromising candidate has inspired more works of art, more social reform, more compassionate action, and more quests for justice than anyone else in history—by far. There are more paintings featuring him, more songs, and books written about him, more good deeds done in his name, more people on the receiving end of rightness because of him than anyone else in the known universe. Ever.

It's hard to wrap our minds round the impact Jesus has made or the levels of interest about him—but at least it's just about believable. What *is* hard to believe is the main reason for him making such an impact. That he was no mere mortal—but God in human flesh.

And, having hit you with such a stark statement from seemingly nowhere, you deserve to have it run past you again. That the reason for the impact Jesus has made is not because he was smarter, cleverer, more passionate, had discovered a few tricks, or had that "extra something." It was that this son of a carpenter was the Creator of the universe who lived with his creation as a real card-carrying member of the human race.

If that claim has holes then millions of people—living and dead—stand condemned of the greatest act of sheer stupidity in the history of the planet. Which, of course, includes me. But if Jesus was, in fact, God arrived in our midst, then no other historical event touches it.

So are we talking about wishful thinking? Or can we find evidence that might convince a sound mind like yours in the way it has mine and zillions like me of every race, color, creed, and star sign?

What Can Support Such a Claim?

Can such a claim possibly stack up? After all, if someone lands on your doorstep saying they are your long-lost cousin—and expecting to be treated as such—you want something more than their words to back up the claim. The same goes for Jesus and his extraordinary declaration to be God.

While the word "God" may be at the top of his resume, are there any points further down the page to help us believe the unthinkable could be true? It's one thing to have people making such a seemingly outrageous statement but could there possibly be any indications that it is not outrageous at all? Let me suggest a few.

His unique ability

If someone were truly God, you would expect them to be able to do things that mere humans couldn't. To be specific, simple "God things" like miracles.

Yes, I know we normal creatures have done some head-spinning stuff. I've seen the shows where David Copperfield and others make tall buildings disappear, turn tigers into Claudia Schiffer, produce people out of top hats, and cut rabbits in half. But we know it's a trick. Somewhere there's a trap door, a mirror or an accomplice.

But the only-God-can-do-them things Jesus did were altogether different. And despite some modern-day protests that they were fiction, such claims were never made at the time—not even by those who wanted his guts for catapult elastic.

After all, up which sleeve did Jesus keep 120 gallons of wine that mysteriously appeared at a wedding? And where did the water it replaced go? Or, if Jesus just used sleight of hand and a little coloring agent, how come the guests who drank it gave it five stars?

In which false compartment did Jesus keep enough bread and fish to feed more than five thousand people in one sitting? And how did he lay on a special effects department to switch off howling gales and torrential rain at the word of his command while on a journey by boat across a lake? In *The Truman Show* maybe, but not in real life.

How did Jesus heal the sickness and crippling conditions of multitudes of people under the eyes of those who had known the sufferers for years? People who knew, for example, that the man now walking had been on his bed for 38 years. And the man now seeing had been blind from the day of his birth.

How did he bring back to life someone who'd been dead so long his grave clothes stank with decay? And how did he walk on water and get someone else to step out of the boat and join him? And how did he . . . The list is endless.

How? If he was no more than flesh and blood, however special, the answer has to be "no way." But if he was God it would be a piece of cake—and quite a lot of loaves and fish.

His teaching focused on himself

If someone was God you would expect what he had to say to be utterly different from others who spoke about spiritual reality—and this was how it was for Jesus.

Other religious leaders directed people's attention to a code of practice or a supreme being. Jesus was entirely different. Almost every time he opened his mouth he spoke about himself. Time and again it was, "I am the good shepherd," "I am the door," "I am the way and the truth and the life." It wasn't simply his words or example Jesus pointed people to—but who he was.

In a mere human, that would put him in the same category as the egomaniac who hijacks every conversation to talk endlessly about himself. You've met them—and don't like them. Jesus was different.

If Jesus were God nothing could be more genuinely important than explaining himself. And to be able to do so without getting up our noses.

He was all we could hope a God would be

If God walked the Earth, what would you want him to be like? And to what extent does Jesus match it? Let me try a few examples on you— just a smattering of all that could be listed if there were time and space to do so.

Jesus was compassionate. Faced with a widowed mother whose only son—and her sole means of support—had died, Jesus raised him to life. Face to face with lepers, the AIDS victims of the day, he did the unthinkable and touched them.

Jesus left no one out. People who lived on the edge of society, social outcasts were all welcomed by him. And women, the underclass of the day, received special affirmation and dignity from the way he treated them.

Jesus made ordinary people feel comfortable in his presence. There was nothing super-religious or standoffish about him. Children swarmed round his feet, he was a welcome guest at a wedding; he enjoyed a normal social life.

Jesus detested religious hypocrisy. He spoke out against those with a better-than-thou attitude. Religion for the show of it stuck in his throat—and he said so.

Jesus never wrote people off. He welcomed those ready for a new start. For example, a prostitute, a thief, and collaborator with the occupying enemy all received the chance to start again. His life expressed what you hope God would be like—that no one is too far gone to be loved by him.

What Did His Friends Think?

Those closest to us know the truth about us. And can have their own way of bringing us down to Earth should we start to loose track of reality. Take my wife for example!

Jesus was no different. He, too, had his own "nearests and dearests." His family and friends. Those who lived cheek by jowl with him for three years listening, watching, and evaluating.

Their verdict? They came to regard him as God—and many went on to give their lives for what they knew to be true. One of them, Thomas, actually knelt at Jesus' feet and declared, "My Lord and my God!" Did Jesus respond with, "Get up, man, I'm nobody's God!" No—instead he freely allowed Thomas to worship him.[2]

Those who knew Jesus well were united in their conviction. Jesus was God.

Jesus Made it Clear He Was God

But you don't only need to make your mind up based on the evidence. You can also take Jesus' own word for it. That's because, in a full on and watch-my-lips way, Jesus stated absolutely clearly that he was God.

That may come as a surprise to you. Because you may have heard the claim that there's no record of Jesus actually saying in words of one syllable "I am God." In a literal sense that's right—but in reality so, so wrong.

It's like this. There I was in a Mexican restaurant waiting for two tons of burritos, tacos, and assorted gunk to arrive. Meanwhile the waiter brought the obligatory nachos and salsa. Looking him straight in the eye I asked, "Is the salsa very hot?" He smiled, winked at my table companions and replied, "Is it hot?!" shrugged his shoulders and walked away.

A moment later a volcano erupted in my mouth. Finally, after much water and perspiration, I protested to my highly amused friends, "He didn't say it was hot!" Which was true—but really.

In the same way, Jesus didn't say in words of one syllable, "I am God." But he left us more clear about the state of play than my Mexican waiter did. He said "I am God" so clearly that to have used the actual words would have been totally unnecessary.

Let me explain what I mean because this really does matter. I am afraid we are back to food again. But this time you are the center of attention. And I hope you like pizza.

It's been a long and hard day and you and your companions are famished. The obvious answer is to have some pizza delivered. So you call Domino's.

Finally the door bell chimes and in front of you is someone in a Domino's uniform. Behind him is his transport, equally Domino's bedecked. And the 15 assorted boxes—including the one with the double chorizo and chilli peppers—tell the same story.

You head to the kitchen where your companions ask, "Was the delivery boy from Domino's?" You reply, "I dunno. He didn't say."

And of course he didn't say. There was no need. In fact, can you imagine if he had actually said, "Good evening, I'm from Domino's Pizza"? You'd feel as though you'd been treated like a monkey in a "How to peel a banana" program. And the same was true for Jesus. He said who he was clearly and plainly, without the need for the actual words, because everything about him left people without a doubt.

So what were the "messages" Jesus sent out that were the equivalent of your mythical pizza delivery boy? What were the words and actions that said "I am God" so clearly it would have seemed strange to have used the words themselves?

Jesus said he and God were one and the same

Jesus spoke of God and himself being one and the same. He made statements like "Anyone who has seen me has seen the Father"[3] and "I and the Father are one."[4]

He also said that to receive him was the same as receiving God; to welcome him was to welcome God.[5]

Jesus spoke of having always existed

When the ancient Jewish leader Moses came face to burning bush with God in the desert, God gave his name as "I AM" to signify that he had always existed. And Jesus used exactly the same phrase when speaking to Jewish leaders telling them, "Before Abraham was born, I am!"[6]

Heard through Jewish ears this claim to be God could be no more blatant than if Jesus had written the words "I am God" in six-foot letters on the side of a house or tattooed them on his forehead.

Jesus forgave people's sin

The Jewish people believed only God could forgive sins. They also believed physical suffering was caused by a person's sin. So, for someone to be healed it meant their sin had been dealt with—something only God could do.

Which meant that when Jesus healed people of disease or disfigurement, he was effectively saying, "I am forgiving sins and healing people—so read me as God."

For example, when a paralyzed man was brought to him, the first thing Jesus said was, "Your sins are forgiven." Then, to prove the point Jesus healed the man—who picked up the portable bed he'd been carried in on and walked away.[7] In both ways his actions proclaimed his identity as boldly as the badge on the pizza boy's outfit.

Indeed, whenever Jesus healed sick people—and he did a lot of it—he sent out the same "I'm God" message. This was blasphemy—a crime punishable by death. Which is why killing him was so high on the agenda of those who rode shotgun on the truth.

Jesus acknowledged the title "Messiah" for himself

For centuries the Jewish people had been looking for "Messiah" to come. The one who would overthrow their enemies and set up a new kingdom in which they could live as free people. This Messiah was referred to in the Old Testament as the "Son of Man"—a title Jesus frequently used about himself.

During Jesus' trial the Jewish high priest asked him, "Are you the Christ [Messiah], the Son of the Blessed One?" Jesus answered, "I am, and you will see the Son of Man sitting at the right hand of the Mighty One and coming on the clouds of heaven."[8]

Because we are not immersed in Jewish culture, the answer Jesus gave may not sound like a statement that he was God. But his questioner was left in no doubt that this reply—full of Jewish imagery—was a claim to be God.

You can be sure of this by what the high priest did next. He ripped his clothes. Not in temper; not in a frothing strop. But because this was the prescribed and traditional response a high priest had to make when faced with an act of blasphemy. And indeed, to his ears he had heard pure unadulterated sacrilege. Jesus claiming to be "The Son of Man," the coming Messiah, said "I am God" just as much as if he had used the exact words.

Jesus said he was God, he did those things you would expect him to do if he were God, and those who were the closest to him believed him. All of which poses all of us with a problem.

What are we to make of someone with dust on his feet and dirt under his fingernails who tells us he is God? Where does it leave us? The answer is, on the horns of a trilemma. Because there are three distinct possibilities. And you have to make a choice.

The Trilemma—One Step Worse than a Dilemma

Someone who says they are God can be only one of three things. They are either 1) A total fruitcake. 2) An absolute fake. Or 3) Telling the truth. In other words they have to be either a lunatic, a liar, or truly the Lord God.

So, which is Jesus?

Jesus the lunatic?

Could Jesus be a lunatic? Because how else do you describe someone who sincerely believes they are God, that they have the authority to forgive sins, and will one day give away seats in heaven?

It reminds me of the official visit to a psychiatric hospital made by the then prime minister, Margaret Thatcher. Introducing herself to one of the patients she said, "Hello, I'm Margaret Thatcher." Came the reply, "Don't worry, dear. I was like that when I came in, but they cured me."

Is this what we must conclude about Jesus? Deluded and to be utterly pitied? That's the only conclusion to be made about someone who claims to be God and who isn't. In which case, does that sound like Jesus to you? Do you see even a hint of someone out of touch with reality and needing to be looked after?

Consider his poise and composure. Weigh up the quality of his life and relationships, the skill and insights of his arguments, and the sheer wisdom that streamed from his lips. Measure the total richness of all he said and did—and its life-enhancing impact throughout history.

Does that sound like the record of someone who went through life completely deluded?

Liar?

But if not a lunatic, could Jesus simply be a liar . . . knowing his statement that he was God was not true but making it anyway?

But just think how much store Jesus put on the need for people to tell the truth. He even said, "The truth shall set you free."[9] Which means he would be more than a liar, he would also be a hypocrite.

In fact, it gets even worse. If he knew he was not God but still said so he would also be an idiot—because it was his claim to be God that led to his death. In other words, he would have been foolish enough to choose to die for something he knew was not true. How dumb is that?

Which leads to the question, "Is it really possible for such insight, wisdom, compassion, and love to come from the life of someone so knowingly deceitful and stupid? Could the greatest and wisest moral teacher in history really be such an immoral and foolish person?"

It would be like discovering Greenpeace owned a nuclear power plant, Sting got rich by owning stock in the weapons industry, Billy Graham had a half share in *Playboy,* or Ralph Nader has all along been in charge of an oil company and recycles diddly squat. But worse!

If, in spite of all that, Jesus was a deliberate liar, we are left with the question "Why?"—because people who are sane lie for only two reasons. Reason 1: To get out of trouble. "Did you do that?" "No" comes the lie—because that's in our best interest. Reason 2: To get an advantage. "Is this yours?" "Yes" comes the lie—for the same reason.

Sane and balanced people lie only because it's to their advantage—to save face, to look more important, to gain what's not theirs, to avoid confrontation, and so on. And for no other reason. In which case, why did this wisest of all teachers choose to lie when he had absolutely nothing to gain—except being nailed to a cross?

Lord God?

So if not a loony or a liar what then? The only other possibility is that Jesus was actually who he claimed to be—God, the Lord of all. This is not an easy conclusion, nor one we can fully understand, but it's the only one which fits the data.

And this is the incredible reality at the heart of the Christian faith. God stepped into first-century dust and dirt to make himself known. God is not hiding; he has made himself plain to see.

Had you been born at the right time you could have shaken the hand of God, talked with him, questioned him, listened to him, watched him, laughed with him, and cried with him. For Jesus is God in a human body.

This is the reason for Jesus' unique impact on history. He came both as God and man. And the waves from that splash are still being felt round the globe and in individual lives.

HEADLINE NEWS

Flimsy rumors or solid evidence?

To be absolutely honest there is another possibility about the identity of Jesus. And you deserve to know.

Perhaps, after all, it's not all down to Jesus being a liar, a lunatic or the Lord God. Supposing what we have been told about him was not true in the first place? To put it bluntly, what if he and his exploits are no more than a legend?

Robin Hood has splashed his merry way across a host of books and films. But there's scant evidence he or any of his bow and arrow exploits ever graced the planet. And will future generations confuse Conan the Barbarian as a genuine figure of history in the same way?

In which case, couldn't Jesus—and all we claim to know about him—be no more than a sophisticated fairy tale? Perhaps the modest exploits of an ancient charismatic figure became exaggerated out of all proportion. And, as a result, the leader became a legend. The man who walked to Jerusalem became a hero who walked on water. The working-class son of Joseph and Mary became the awesome Son of God.

Or perhaps it is really all down to some Jewish religious fanatics needing a Messiah and inventing him. Or them being deluded enough to believe Jesus to be God and so writing him up as doing the things they expected God to do.

It is only honest to ask if these explanations could make sense of the seemingly unbelievable claims made about Jesus. Did he really turn water into wine, heal all kinds of diseases, and even bring dead people back to life? Was Jesus truly God or could it all be exaggeration, confusion, and myth?

It may seem a strange way to respond to questions like these but it is time to head for the kitchen—and to ask for a loan of your imagination.

Spread before you are the personal papers of your recently deceased Aunt Fiona. And there it is, the long lost recipe for the magnificent quadruple-jam-layered triple-chocolate upside-down cake that's been the talk of your family for years.

The original creator was your mother's aunt's great-grandfather's uncle's cousin's sister. It was handed down by word of mouth and finally committed to paper. Then copied many times, with one of those copies being in your hands right now.

You dash to the kitchen screaming, "That cake will live again!" And, in your skilled hands, it will.

But suppose, in the telling and copying, the recipe has changed down the generations? What you now hold is not the real thing. Journey from mouth to ear to mouth to ear to mouth to . . . has done its damage. And enthusiastic kin decided such a fine recipe deserved to be improved. As a result, somewhere along the line, six eggs have gradually become 16. Fifteen minutes have turned into five hours. Jam has become spam.

There's only one way to find out—and that's to make the cake. And you do. The result? Magnificardo! The recipe works! It's so good you want to dive in and swim. To invite your friends, neighbors, and the whole world to have a taste.

So now back to the real issue at hand. Has the "recipe" about Jesus changed or been messed with along the way? If that's what has happened, the proof of this cake is going to be in the eating. With those who take Jesus at his word being left with a very nasty taste.

But the exact opposite is true.

Today—and for centuries past—people of every walk of life and of almost every language and nation have put the message of Jesus to the test and found it works. They have lived and died by it. They have discovered a fullness to life, real peace of mind and confidence in the ultimate future.

Which means there's a more appropriate question than "Is what we know accurate?" It's "How come what we know from all that time ago is still accurate?" And the answer is brain-numbingly simple.

The Gospels

What we know about the life of Jesus comes mainly from four accounts of his life known as the Gospels. They were written by four of his most committed followers. They were either eyewitnesses themselves—like Matthew and John—or they got the story straight from those who saw Jesus firsthand—like Mark and Luke.

They had reasons to get it right

To them, the words and deeds of Jesus—and the events surrounding his life, death, and resurrection—were too important to be casual about. In a way, they had the same concerns as Jewish historians asked to report on the Holocaust. The importance of the events made them doubly committed to accuracy in every detail.

If that wasn't the case then they would have told a very different story. They would have been sure to leave out the things that presented those who followed Jesus in a bad light or didn't suit their argument. But they didn't.

As a result of their "accuracy matters most" attitude

- They told of the way the disciples abandoned Jesus in his hour of greatest need and of one of them who swore blind he'd never met him.
- They admitted to the disciples' bumbling attempts to make head or tail of what Jesus was on about and of their inner arguments about who was the greatest.
- They even include Jesus' family saying they thought he was out of his mind and Jesus' seeming cry of defeat on the cross, "Father, why have you abandoned me?"[10]
- They told of women being the first witnesses of Jesus coming alive again—when women were dismissed as second-class citizens and not allowed to give evidence in a court of law.

Moreover, these eyewitness recorders were not simple peasants—those who, when offered the opportunity to drink at the fount of knowledge, chose only to gargle. Instead they included a former civil servant, a businessman, and a doctor.

They were sophisticated enough to eventually travel to most of the known world—playing a part in transforming it. And so convinced as to the truth of what they wrote they went on to give their lives for it.

They had multitudes of others to keep them on track

Better still, the Gospel writers had far more than their own observations and memories to go on. Jesus was "THE" event. A large group of people began to follow him around, hanging on everything he said and did. They saw people cared for, the sick healed, families transformed, relationships enriched, lives dramatically changed.

At that time it was all as exciting and public as Janet Jackson's "wardrobe malfunction" at the Super Bowl, or Bill Clinton's "I never . . ." in the White House.

And, of course, people then were just as able to recall their own vivid experiences. Do you remember where and how you heard about the death of Princess Diana or the fall of the Twin Towers? I do—in widescreen surround-sound detail.

If you think about it, you have seen the way people have amazing recall years later about significant events. Almost every time there's an anniversary of some not-too-distant historic event, the news media get those who were present to tell their version. And, time and time again, these eyewitness versions are an exact match to the historical record.

In Jesus' day this was even more true. His was what sociologists call an aural culture, one where storytelling was the TV of the day. With people using their memories to the full so as to keep track of their history and traditions. Which was how information traveled great distances both geographically and down the ages.

This meant the Gospel writers were surrounded by people with vivid memories. Memories of seeing a man everyone knew had been blind from birth receive the gift of sight. People who had heard teaching which made a direct cruise missile strike on their hearts. People who, every time they got together, would go over what Jesus had said or done.

"Did you hear that? The story about the son who ran away—that was a killer!"

"Yes—remember the bit about him eating what was left over from the pigs? But hey, were you standing there later when he healed that woman? She just touched his cloak, and was as right as rain. She'd been going to doctors for 12 years and they hadn't done a thing for her!"

Some—those who spent the most time with Jesus—even memorized the stories he told and the teachings he gave. Because this was what followers of a rabbi did in those days.

They had enemies waiting to pounce

Matthew, Mark, Luke, and John couldn't have had it easier to get the "recipe" down right. But they also got help from a very unexpected quarter— their enemies. Watching from the wings were those who hated this mushrooming movement. Those ready to pounce on any distortion or exaggeration. They dared not get it wrong.

Had any of the Gospel writers disappeared into the desert for a few months to create their manuscript in splendid isolation it would have been far from splendid. Good perhaps but not good enough. It could have be like leaving your Great Uncle John to tell his hunting and fishing stories without the scrutiny of those who knew what really happened.

But that's not how it was. Friends and enemies kept the writers on track—making sure their memories and those of many others did not wobble on the way.

Okay, so if that's how the record of Jesus' life came to be written down, how come it remained accurate down through the centuries?

No time for mythtakes

The accounts of what Jesus said and did were committed to writing too soon after the events for them to become blown up into a myth.

It was only five or so years after Jesus' death that letters were circulating among his followers containing the central events of his life. And those who earn their crust studying such things insist that the Gospels themselves were written during the lifetime of people who knew Jesus personally.

That is just far too short a time for distortions to turn a man into a God. Legends like that of King Arthur of Camelot took centuries to take shape.

Lots of Copies Exist

There were soon lots of copies to compare with each other for accuracy. As the result of being persecuted for what they believed, the first believers became scattered far and wide. This meant they needed to keep in touch with the great story. As a result, soon hundreds of copies of the things Jesus said and did went into circulation. And they all matched.

Today there are literally thousands of such manuscripts and when copies from different eras are compared they match time after time. Which isn't surprising either, because those who copied "the recipe" cared as much about its accuracy as those who had written it in the first place.

It wasn't a case of finding some "man-wlth-pen" copy-stand where some guy on cheap labor churned out a few manuscript "replicas" based on how he felt at the time. Those who created the manuscripts did so with the same dedicated commitment to their accuracy as the original writers.

There's even something more

But even above all this there is something more—which you can choose to believe or not. It is that the Gospel records are more than just words on paper but one of the special ways God has chosen to make himself known.

This is not the place to blow your mind with the amazing history of the Bible—of which the Gospels are part. It would take more space than we have to enthrall you with the amazing story of the way the Bible has survived every attempt to remove it or attack it. Or to give you the endless stories of lives changed through its impact. But, that being the case, you are left with the Gospels being more than the work of committed writers doing their very best.

Rather, the God who made everything—from galaxies to atoms—wants the Gospels to do more than record history but to convey a personal and powerful message to all who encounter them.

Millions of people have already reached the conclusion that the Gospels can be trusted. Some have done so simply on faith. Others have sifted the evidence with painstaking thoroughness.

Those who have believed after checking the facts carefully include some of the most eminent scientists, scholars, academics, and thinkers of the day—with IQs the size of telephone numbers.

So Why Do People Still Doubt the Gospels?

Yet if it is as obvious as all this you may wonder why, despite the impressive evidence for the record of the life of Jesus, you still hear people say extraordinary things in order to dismiss it.

What you'll find, time and again, is that historians—those who deal in making sense of the past—will tell you the Gospels are an amazing record of history. In their eyes, diligent witnesses set it all out with care, archaeology supports what they wrote and we are inundated with good copies of the manuscripts to show they have not been meddled with during the passage of time.

Historians will line up to tell you that the records of Jesus' life outshine those of any other comparable figure in history.

Who are those who struggle with the events recorded in the Gospels? Not historians but theologians—those who make their living working out what God is like. They are not scientists but thinkers, some of whom have a preconceived idea as to what is allowed to happen in the universe and how God should behave.

That means when the historical record says something they have never seen happen or they don't think could happen they make their own judgment against the hard evidence. In their terms, the things written down are impossible so there must be another explanation. And the explanation they like is that it is not true.

This begs a simple but profound question: "If God had come to Earth as Jesus, lived among ordinary people, done extraordinary things, suffered a criminal's death and come to life three days later, what evidence would have been left behind?"

Disbelieving theologians say, "I don't like the question!" Open-minded historians say, "The Gospels, of course."

The Gospels record events that may seem beyond belief. And we may find it hard to accept they happened, judged against what happens in the average shopping mall on a Monday morning. But the authentic nature of the gospel record means we can be absolutely confident that the version of Jesus' life found there can be trusted.

That includes the belief that history's most astounding event actually took place. Three days after he was certified dead, Jesus came alive again. And that's where we are going next.

BOO!

No longer dead and buried?

Just when the authorities were uncorking the champers, convinced this upstart preacher was no more—he pops up again. Here, there, and everywhere! No longer dead and buried but walking, talking, and even eating—at least, according to his followers.

Having been thoroughly executed and hermetically sealed in a tomb, the word on the street is, Jesus is alive and in remarkably good health.

Beyond belief? Not to those who saw it with their own eyes. And not to the billions who have trusted their story ever since.

Can It Really be True?

Historians see the resurrection of Jesus as one of the most authenticated events in ancient history. But in recent times others have thrown up a whole handful of theories to explain it away.

Some say Jesus never really died but just passed out. Later, after the shade of the tomb cooled him off, he dusted himself down and said "Boo" to the world. Others say that Jesus' body was stolen right from under the noses of the guards—so his followers could just pretend he had risen again.

Still others claim Jesus' followers must have gone to the wrong place. Hysterical and confused, they simply turned left instead of right and got overly excited about the wrong tomb being empty.

And then there's those who would say it was all in the mind. The disciples were hallucinating together or were only speaking "figuratively" when they said they saw him.

Could any of these possibilities make sense of it all? It's easy to check. Hop on the Enterprise, hit warp factor seven and land at the time it was all happening. Did I say easy? The other way is to let the culture of the times and the eyewitness accounts recorded in the Gospels speak for themselves.

Was Jesus still alive when he left the cross?

What would the Roman soldier in charge of the execution crew at the time tell us?

Based on the way crucifixions were conducted and what the Gospel writers tell us, it would be something like: "At a crucifixion it's my job to make sure they're dead—really dead. Only then will the officials release the body for burial. I've done hundreds of crucifixions—and never got it wrong. Wouldn't dare to. The mistake would cost me my life. And we had to keep a special eye on this one. Any doubt he wasn't dead and I'd have done to him what I did to the two on either side of him—broke their legs so they choked to death on their own weight.[11] But I knew he'd had it. Especially when I stabbed my spear into his heart and all that blood and stuff ran out. Was he dead? One hundred percent. He couldn't have been anything else."[12]

Or let's let Joseph of Arimathea, the follower of Jesus who looked after the burial, have his say.

"Not dead? Woke up in the tomb and made his own way out? That has to be fantasy—because we followed Jewish burial customs to the letter. First we washed the body. And dead bodies just feel different. Then we wrapped it with linen grave clothes, starting at the feet and working upwards. Then we applied 75 pounds of aloe and myrrh—a thick and pungent gooey tree resin—which glued it all together.[13] We left, pulling out the wedge holding back a huge stone which then rolled down the slope into position to cover the grave-opening. And the authorities sealed it and placed a guard unit outside to keep troublemakers and thieves away. To escape, Jesus would have needed to rip his way out of 75 pounds of super-glued cloth, single-handedly roll a two-ton stone back up an incline and then kung fu fight his way through a group of highly trained and armed Roman soldiers.

"That's beyond belief!"

Was it a grave mistake?

What would Jesus' close friend Mary Magdalene tell us? She and another woman were the first to find the tomb empty.

"When I went there I didn't expect to see anything else other than Jesus' body. But here was the tomb—empty. I could only think that the officials had taken his body away somewhere. But then Jesus himself came to me, called me by name, and tried to calm me down."[14]

Let's let Jesus' friend Peter take up the story:

"Mary's news sent me racing to the tomb. And I couldn't believe it! I was expecting to meet a group of soldiers but instead found an empty tomb. Inside there was no body—only the heavy, sticky grave clothes— left behind by someone who was obviously very much alive. That's what first convinced us that he raised himself from the dead, passing through garments that weighed as much as three boxes of fish.[15] Did we go to the wrong tomb? You don't forget where you bury the most important person in your life. Anyway, how did the grave clothes get there if I went to the wrong place?"

Was it all in the mind?

Let's say your car has just had a very considerable argument with a brick wall—and lost. Next stop is the junkyard. Since you don't expect it will ever run again you strip off the plugs, points, wheels, and a few other rattly bits.

But what if you had some wild hope that the fairy-car-mother would somehow appear and restore the wreck and deliver it to your door in mint condition three days later?

If you believed that, you would do all you could to help. You would leave everything as whole and unbroken as possible. But as you have no such expectation—you strip it bare and walk away.

This is exactly the attitude the disciples showed to the body of Jesus—but with considerably more respect. They had no expectation of a grand finale. No hope of him rising from the dead. So they buried him using all that cloth and gloop to truss him up and weigh him down. By encasing Jesus in a suit of hardened gunk, we know they never expected his body to move again.

In which case, perhaps a few coincidences—a couple of people thinking they saw Jesus—were blown up out of all proportion? Not at all.

The sightings of Jesus we are invited to believe are not based on a fleeting glimpse by a few of people on a hot afternoon after a very liquid lunch. Nor is this about an isolated sighting of Adolf Hitler on a beach in some Central American city, or Elvis on a porch in Hawaii.

Or could it all have been an illusion?

There was nothing brief or casual about the contact the disciples had with the risen Jesus. It amazes people to discover how many saw him. Over a period of about forty days they couldn't stop bumping into Jesus. It happened all over the place—on the road walking, in a private room, on top of a hill, by the side of a lake.

And these weren't quick two-minute "How's your father" conversations. They talked and talked together—about the way the Jewish scriptures had foretold his life, about their own personal needs, and about his future plans for them. On and on and on.

Jesus appeared to a vast range of people in a wide array of circumstances, who can't all have simply been overcome with emotion and a touch of the vapors.

- At least ten people locked in a room together were terrified when the unexpected happened and Jesus appeared among them.[16]
- Cleopas and his friend on the Emmaus road were gobsmacked when the man who joined them turned out to be Jesus and started to share dinner with them.[17]
- Thomas will go down in history as "the doubter," because he absolutely refused to believe until he met Jesus face to face. Jesus then invited him to touch the places on his hands where the nails had gone in.[18]
- All the disciples were fishing early when Jesus showed up on the beach. Peter, extremely excited, jumped in and swam ashore while the rest rowed in to share a nice breakfast of smoked kippers with Jesus.[19]
- Then there was the crowd of 500 that the risen Jesus appeared to—all at the same time—all hearing him share the same message.[20]

In each case Jesus took time to give those involved what they needed at that moment—comfort, reassurance, explanation, physical evidence.

And the details, which were recorded by the Gospel writers, sound absolutely genuine. There's no ring of something churned out as the religious party line. Or of fanciful embellishment.

Did They Die For a Lie?

Maybe the followers of Jesus just made it all up. Somehow they managed to steal the body from under the noses of the Romans, buried him secretly, and began pumping out the "He is risen!" message. And fame and fortune awaited.

But almost all of those early followers of Jesus met painful, unpleasant deaths—inflicted because they believed Jesus was alive and kept on saying so. If they knew it was a lie they were among the most stupid people ever to have lived. For who is dumb enough to give their life for a cause they know to be based on a lie?

Instead, the reality of the resurrection transformed their lives completely. I'm thinking about people like Peter, Paul, and John.

- Peter, a hot-tempered fisherman, was once so scared of being arrested with Jesus he swore and lied his way out of trouble, denying he ever knew him. Belief in the resurrection made Peter a bold, outspoken leader of the early Christians. It's said he died by being crucified upside down.
- Paul, a highly educated Jewish rabbi, was once determined to wipe out all traces of those who believed. Then he came face to face with the resurrected Jesus. Soon he was traveling throughout the known world telling people the news. Tradition tells us he was beheaded by the Roman emperor Nero.
- John, Jesus' close friend, was also a fisherman and nicknamed "Son of Thunder" because of his quick temper. Through the impact of the resurrection he became a leader of the early Christians, and died in exile.

These are but an infinitesimal fraction of all who have risked life and limb for their belief in Jesus and his resurrection—both then and now.

What Transformed These Ordinary People?

Think back to the scene where Jesus breathed his last. Huddled under the feet of their dying leader stood a rag-tag, discouraged bunch of wannabes. It was all over but the burial. High hopes didn't pan out. It was great while it lasted. But now he's dead. Time to go back home, pick up the pieces and keep clear of all those who will say, "I told you so."

The hopes the disciples had of co-ruling in Jesus' new Kingdom had been crushed. All the aspirations of personal fame and fortune lay in tatters. More than that, they were sure those who killed Jesus had them as next-to-be-eaten on the dinner list.

They didn't even have courage to flee the city. They hid huddled in a room, cowering behind locked door and closed shutter. In fear of their lives, with their morale devastated. They had lost it all.

Yet only weeks later we find that these very same cowards are out in the open, fit to busting, and telling all who will listen about the living Jesus raised from the dead by the power of God.

Something had so electrified and transformed the followers of Jesus, that faith in him swept the length and breadth of the Roman Empire in the next 300 years. What one single event could bring about such a transformation? Jesus truly rising from the dead.

British journalist Mark Tully revisited the scene of Jesus' life interviewing people for a BBC TV series on Jesus. It ended with his own view. He said, "That man was probably a failure in his own time . . . He taught in strange riddles. He didn't convince his fellow Jews. And he didn't overthrow Rome.

"From that failure I have come to what, for me, is the most important conclusion of all. That the hardest, apparently least historical article of Christian faith, the resurrection, must have happened. If there had been no miracle after Jesus' death, there would have been no grounds for faith in a failed life. No resurrection . . . no Church."

Dare We Believe?

It's one thing for eyewitnesses to believe such a startling thing happened. But surely we can't be expected to. Yet why not? Throughout life we take actions on the basis of the words of those who have seen when we haven't.

I've just had the flat roof on the very top of my three-storey house resurfaced at the cost of a small fortune. And all because I believed the testimony of the expert who climbed up to have a look. I didn't ask for a photograph, ten other witnesses, or a section to be brought down for inspection.

The eyewitness had all the credentials of an honest man, offered a cast-iron guarantee, and had everything to lose if I found him to be taking me for a ride. And so I believed.

I wasn't around 2,000 years ago to see the resurrected Jesus for myself. But along with millions of others I have taken the word of those who were. The evidence is simply too overwhelming to believe anything else.

7

BLINDED BY THE LIGHT

Coming to terms with who God is

So God turned up on planet Earth and started to talk. And when the Supreme fount of all knowledge and wisdom starts to flow, significant things are said.

Of course, the temptation for Jesus' listeners was to look for the "what's in it for me" content. Like "Can you make sure we get the best seats in heaven?" "Can you roast our enemies?" And "Can you feed us for ever?"

But Jesus had more important things on his lips. He wanted the people then—and now—to be crystal clear about how to squeeze the maximum juice out of life and what to do with the leftover peels.

In fact, Jesus said it plain and simple—no doubt with a big smile on his face—"I've come so you can have life to the very full."[21] And then told people exactly how that life could be theirs.

For most of us, "life" is simply "life." The cards each of us are dealt may be different from those others get—but it's still just "life." The thought that there's another kind of life, one that's "life to the very full" may have passed you by. In which case please consider my friend Joseph's very strange ears for a moment.

Most normal people's ear canals go straight into their head—but not Joseph—he always has to be spectacularly different. His earholes go in, take a sharp turn up and then turn in again. Why give you this piece of seemingly irrelevant information? Because it explains why, for long periods, Joseph hears next to nothing. His weird earholes gather wax at an alarming rate—creating waxy brown plugs closely resembling cigar butts and making him nearly deaf.

But then comes an amazing moment for Joseph. When he makes his annual visit to the ear-igator who hits him with the earhole version of colonic irrigation, his whole world changes. Life is now as it is meant to be in the hearing department—full, rich, vibrant. For months Joseph had chugged on thinking this was how life was meant to be. But then came "hearing in all its fullness."

What Jesus came to bring was something like that—not just for our ears—but for the whole of our being. He came so we could have life the way it was meant to be—full.

A Whole New Life

Obviously Joseph is not oblivious to his hearing deficiency. He can sense the symptoms and, at times, count the bruises. And that's how it is when it comes to life. Not that life can't be good—even great—sometimes. But deep down, for most of us, we sense there is more of life to be experienced, more of living to be realized, more of love to be known.

And it's a serious issue. After all, life is the most precious thing we possess and we only get one shot. There's no dress rehearsal. No rewind, erase and "let's try that again." Jesus wanted to deliver the key to living life to the full; for us experiencing a deep inner satisfaction that lasts. He came to change our lives from "just getting by" into "being really alive."

A Whole New Kingdom

The way Jesus spoke about it was as though people can become citizens of a totally different kind of kingdom—the Kingdom of God. Its citizens are to be those who enjoy the true inner peace that comes from knowing they have a clean slate, a fresh start with God and each other. In this Kingdom, God is King and people live under his protection and in his ways.

The invitation Jesus made to be a citizen of God's Kingdom—and experience life to the full—is open to all. An "all" that includes the crushed and broken, the deprived and vulnerable, the weak and powerless, those who suffer for doing what is right, and those who, all along, have wanted to know God.

And Jesus was as good as his words. As could be seen through the kind of lives Jesus impacted—including the rich and famous, military generals, the religious elite and hoards of regular working people. But that was not the end of it. Those Jesus invited included people regarded as total scum by everyone else. Jesus' Kingdom of God has room for drunkards, prostitutes, thieves, traitors, murderers, and more. Anyone who wants more from life and is willing to accept they can't get it on their own.

Jesus' invitation was simple. He said, "Come as you are as long as you know that's not the way you ought to be."

Knowing What God Is Like

However, all who heard Jesus already had their eyes wide open to something vital; and it's something we may easily miss. They had been taught from early on what God is truly like. They knew better than to imagine God as a gentle force or being who didn't have to be reckoned with. Like a puppy dog. Safe, agreeable, and okay to take on—no matter what.

They knew God's essence, what he is made up of, to be far from safe and agreeable. Not because he is nasty, cruel or vindictive. But because of the very substance of what he is.

Let me try to explain what that means.

Day by day you sit within reach of an electric socket and don't give it a second thought. Of course you are careful. No "let's see what happens if I stick my fingers in here while standing in a bowl of water" stuff from you. But you happily use electricity to run your appliances.

But there's a bigger picture than this. Somewhere, probably many miles from you, a huge power station is generating raw, naked, electrical power. This electricity is nothing like the few meager watts that help keep your hair curled, your model train chuffing or your toaster toasting. This is "power" with a capital "POW."

And what if that kind of electricity went straight into your home? It would be meltdown in all its fullness. Wires would fizzle. Light bulbs would pop. Appliances would melt. Your home would be left as a charred blob on the landscape.

To get my drift try plugging a US device into a European electrical socket—which delivers twice the juice of a US socket. Joseph still has the stench of the resulting white smoke ingrained in the memory of his nostrils from when he did that to his PC. He'd also still be hearing the crackling as it fried, had it not been for his waxy ears.

We can all too easily assume the great God of the universe to be like common domestic electricity. Tame. Safe. Manageable. But those who heard Jesus' offer to follow him knew God to be like the raw power that comes from the electricity plant.

The ancients even had a technical word for this kind of power— "holy." God is holy. Pure, powerful, and unspoiled goodness. A search-light, not a flashlight. A forest fire, not a flickering match. A tsunami, not a wave.

And "holy" consumes anything that is not of the same substance—in the same way darkness is consumed by light, forests are consumed by fire, and whole swathes of land are consumed by a tsunami.

Imagine a wave 1,000 times higher, bigger, and more powerful than the terrible Indian Ocean tsunami of Christmas 2004. It is but water and yet everything that gets in its way as it passes over is devastated, demolished, and destroyed. Everything, that is, which is not like it— which is not water itself.

In a way, God is like that. Of course God is a personal being. But imagine his very make-up as an unlimited powerful wave of energy. Anything or anyone who comes into contact with him, but is not like him, is destroyed—just like a powerful tsunami destroys anything that is not water.

That's what those listening to Jesus knew. And the first step to living that "life in all its fullness" is to know it too.

Knowing What We Are Like

Those who heard Jesus also knew the truth about what they were really like. And it was that they were the very opposite of what God is like. God is goodness through and through. Pure and perfect in every way to the millionth degree and then some. And they most definitely were not. Selfishness, pride, dishonesty, and the rest all infests the human condition—their condition and ours. And they knew it.

Just as they had a technical word to describe what God was like—"holy"— they had a word to sum up what they were like—"sinful." And they knew the problem this left them with when it came to wanting to get close up and comfortable with God. Just as balloons and pins are best kept apart, as are gas and an open flame, so God's absolute purity has a devastating impact on our own sinfulness.

Think of it this way. Ever lifted a rock and seen the insects that are suddenly exposed to the shattering blaze of the sun fleeing for cover? This is what it would be like for us to suddenly be exposed to God's holy presence—his power, light, and purity would expose our nakedness and blow us away.

To get our own heads round this we have to admit the word "sin" is much misunderstood. It brings to mind wagging fingers and miserable killjoys in black suits standing on soap boxes and bellowing judgment at all who pass by. We picture the stern-faced lord of the manor turning away the unmarried waif with her newborn child. Back into the black night she must go, condemned never to darken the door again.

Yet "sin" is the perfect word to describe what causes us to be blinded by the light of God's presence. But don't think of it so much about a list of things we do. Rather, first and foremost, think of it as a description of our human condition.

For example, have you ever been in charge of a shopping cart that spent its time charging into stacks of food no matter how hard you tried to steer it? The symptoms of the problem can be seen in the dents made in people or produce. But it's the condition of the cart and its bent wheel that is the real problem.

In the same way, I have a son who suffers from asthma. You'll see him show all the signs of his condition like using a little "puffer" from time to time, or stopping to catch his breath. These are just two of the symptoms of his condition.

Just as the shopping cart by nature chooses to go its own way, and my son is by nature an asthmatic, we are, by nature, sinful and our condition has symptoms. The "condition" is to be drawn to do those things and think those things we shouldn't. And the "symptoms" are the wrong ways we think and wrong things we do.

It Wasn't Me. Well, Okay, It Was

Like Little Red Riding Hood, we all have a given set of rules to go by. Hers were simple.

- Don't talk to wolves—or any other strangers.
- Be nice to Grandma.
- Deliver the goods.
- Get home safely.

Our rules are best expressed in the Ten Commandments—God's non-negotiables for life at its best. Most of us know them—things like, don't lie, don't steal, don't commit adultery. The problem is we treat the Ten Commandments as though they were ten suggestions—or as a range of options on a KFC menu. We are as effective in obeying as was the kid with the red hood on her journey to Grandma's house.

Like Red Riding Hood, we have a choice. We can do things the way God wants them done, or the way we want to do them.

Our basic attitude is to steadfastly choose to go our own sweet, and not so sweet, way rather than God's way. We habitually think of ourselves first and others last. And even some of the best things we do are designed more to make us feel better about who we are than to help others.

Think of it as though God created us with the ability to play darts and hit the bull's-eye every time. But now, we can't even hit the board—we're so off target there are holes all over the wall. And this is true in every area of our life when seen from God's perspective. We constantly fall short, fail to make the grade, and miss the mark.

Why does it matter? Because God's rules are not of the "Keep off the grass" and "No ball games in the pool" variety. They are for the best interest of everyone and everything—our own self included. When we break God's wise rules we damage our relationship with him, injure ourselves and hurt others.

Yet these are far more than rules. They are the very fiber of society and the universe. To break them is to betray the one who made us.

Jesus summed them up—love God and everyone else.

Purple Passages

It may surprise you to know that Jesus hardly mentioned the issue of "sin" to ordinary people. Instead, his purple passages on the subject were saved for those who thought they were the finished article. Those convinced their religious rituals made them pure and holy enough for God to tick their box.

Jesus reserved a splendid vocabulary for people like this. His charm offensive included calling them a "brood of vipers," "hypocrites," and "whitewashed tombs . . . full of dead men's bones."[22]

Sadly they'd lost the plot. They thought "almost perfect" was the pass mark. But in the blaze of God perfection it's a different picture. Even the smallest blemish can spoil everything. Sin can be like just one oily thumbprint on a pure white wedding gown. It spoils everything.

How small a smear of dishwashing soap needs to be left on your cup to make your coffee undrinkable? How much damage to a load of white washing can one very small red sock inflict? How many salmonella germs does it take to close a restaurant?

Those who saw themselves as "good enough" got it with both verbal barrels. Yet when around ordinary people, Jesus stayed tight-lipped on the issue of sin—because they knew they didn't match up to God's holiness and didn't need to be yelled at about it.

We, too, know our own self-centeredness inflicts sadness, pain, and disappointment on others. We know how often we fall short of our own standards. And be thankful that modern technology still excludes a machine capable of projecting our innermost thoughts onto a big screen for all to see.

We have an innate sense that we don't measure up to what God wants us to be. Of course, we have some sharp ways to hide it. Nifty phrases like "But I'm as good as the next person" can keep us from thinking the whole thing through with reality. But that only works so long as that "next person" isn't Jesus.

Because of our condition we can never match what God expects of us. Look at it this way. Do you ever remember going into a store to buy a new pair of shoes while feeling pretty good about the pair you were wearing at the time? And cringing when the pair you tried on made the old look so shabby you couldn't even bear to wear them home?

Having seen perfection, we discovered our previously perfectly acceptable shoes were not so perfect after all.

It is similar when we compare what we are inside to what God expects of us. Most of the time we feel pretty good about ourselves. In our eyes, compared with most people, we are "pretty good, thank you." And compared with some others, God should be grateful to have us on his planet. We're okay.

But God has a different standard. It's a "new shoes" standard. It's one to match who he is and what he created. It's the standard of absolute moral goodness, purity, and perfection—and it's the standard we are measured against. Which means, in his eyes we are like damaged goods well past their sell-by date.

Little Red Riding Hood's behavior sounds a lot like that described by the prophet Isaiah when he wrote, "We all, like sheep, have gone astray, each of us has turned to his own way . . ."[23] We may have stamped our hooves and bleated "shan't." Or just wandered off, enticed by seemingly better things. But in both cases, sin has equally serious consequences. We need to understand what it is that sin does—to us, to others, and to God himself.

Seeing Through the Smog

We were created to know God and enjoy his company for ever. But sin has become a barrier between us.

Sin is the cloud, the smog, between us and God. It's what separates us from experiencing the warmth of his love. The prophet Isaiah puts it like this: "your iniquities have separated you from your God; your sins have hidden his face from you . . ."[24] How come? Because like oil and water, God's holiness and our sinfulness don't mix.

But we are tempted to ask why can't God be a little more understanding about our sin? Couldn't he turn a blind eye and lower the pass mark a little? Such thoughts show we haven't even begun to grasp the seriousness of the situation. He simply knows what's best for his world, including us.

Don't picture God as an over-eager policeman at his happiest when making people miserable. You will see in the following pages, the very opposite is true.

In reality, it could be said that sin is its own judge and reaps its own rewards. That this is the natural outcome when light meets darkness. The light always reveals what is true. Let me try to illustrate what I mean.

I was proud of our lawn. The bits worn thin by the children's paddling pool had grown back. At long last it was verge-to-verge green and splendid—except for just the occasional weed. Or so I thought.

A neighbor offered some of his spare "Weed and Feed" and I was soon depositing it across my treasured possession in a nifty dispenser on wheels. "It can only look even better," I told myself.

Within days the truth was revealed, as large brown dead patches spread everywhere across what I had believed was near perfection. Judgment day had come and the truth was out. What had looked so good to my untrained eye had been the right color but the wrong substance. Moss, clover, and some stuff with odd Latin names had withered under the impartial evaluation of something that knew the difference between grass and weeds.

That's how it will be when we stand before God—as each of us surely will one day. In the searching gaze of his perfect evaluation, what seems so okay to us will be revealed in all its shabbiness and poverty. Why? Because that is what is right and fair.

Did I say something about fair?

Don't Worry, God Is Fair

There is much more to God than him being our judge.

Standing before a school assembly I asked the children to list the components of the perfect parent. Once "rich" and "generous" were out of the way, they got to the serious stuff—like "fair." Then came my loaded question, "Do you expect to be punished when you step out of line?" The reply was unanimous and loud—"Oh no!!"

Then came loaded question number two. "So if your brother or sister beats up on you or breaks your things they should go unpunished too?" Dilemma and confusion struck.

They wanted a parent who is both fair and unfair at the same time. And it's the same with us. We want God to put an end to wrong—so long as his actions don't cramp our style or have personal implications. We want him to step in and take care of all the bad things that happen in this world, but at the same time to leave us alone to do whatever we want.

But if God is to be fair he must deal with sin—including ours.

So how can that happen? What could God possibly do that would make him both fair and forgiving at the same time? How can he act with justice while showing love and compassion?

Don't despair. Because God is committed to providing us with life in all its fullness. He has provided a way to rescue us and deliver us to permanent safety and security. And that's where we are headed next.

CRIME OF PASSION

Executed? But wasn't he such a nice boy?

If you capsized while canoeing in a North Carolina river, figure on a $3,500 bill to bail you out. Try not to get lost while skiing in Vermont, because someone has to pay the $10,000 in loose change it would take to help you find your way back to the lodge. Before climbing Mt McKinley make sure to keep in mind the cost of keeping you from becoming a human icicle—a mere $50,000 to $200,000—depending on where you get stuck. But that doesn't even scratch a recent rescue of two from a doomed yacht in the icy waters off the coast of New Zealand—try NZ$1,000,000 for size.

Rescue and recovery is a very expensive business, but you may be relieved to know that those on the receiving end don't normally get stuck with the bill. It's more than likely taxpayers or philanthropists who foot the majority of a rescue bill.

But if you think rescuing humans from dangerous sports is expensive, be glad you're not an amphibian. Fifty international amphibian experts have just asked for $400 million to help save the planet's frogs, toads, newts, and salamanders because of the crisis caused by the current global-warming climate. And another project in Sonoma County, California has also put a $400 million price tag on saving just their local species—the California Tiger Salamander.

And while your eyes may roll around in your head while thinking about the huge cost of saving a skier or a salamander, hold your breath for the cost of rescue and recovery for the most expensive natural disaster in American history. According to the US Social Security Department the price tag for rescuing and helping to recover those who suffered under the terrible onslaught wrought by Hurricane

Katrina was $150 billion—$25 million of which was given to help save the hurricane's animal victims.

And why spend so much to rescue one person or a group of people or even our pets from sure and certain demise? Because we matter. We matter to those who love us. We matter to one another. And as corny as it may sound—we especially matter to God.

We can put a value on the cost of getting plucked from death's jaws whether on a mountainside or from a river—or even from a devastating hurricane or tsunami. But what about the cost of rescuing ourselves from ourselves and the awful things we sometimes do to others?

The answer to that question lies in two pieces of wood laid over one another to form a simple cross.

The Cross as a Symbol

Symbols are powerful communicators. Companies spend into the tens of thousands in creating, copyrighting, and getting into public view, an icon that represents their persona. They want something that conveys the essence of who they are.

For McDonald's it's the golden arches. For Nike it's the tick. American Express uses the face of a Trojan. While for Apple it's the, errr . . . apple.

The message is, "Look at this. Think of us."

If symbols are so important, how come the one most often used by those who follow Jesus is a cross? Why go for an image most people know is a blatant link to the bloody and barbaric death of Jesus?

Couldn't they find something more consumer-friendly? A bunch of loaves and fishes, a footprint on water, a hand patting a child's head, or a star in the sky? But not a cross. Who would buy into a product rep-resented by a symbol of torture and slow, painful death? It's like a com-pany today using a hangman's noose or an electric chair as their logo.

So what is it about a cross that makes it so central to everything the followers of Jesus believe and stand for? And what's it got to do with me?

The answer is simple. Today people wear crosses but 2,000 years ago, crosses wore people. That included Jesus. It was his death on a cross that formed the focus of attention for his followers and explains to us the significance of why he came.

This deserves an extra paragraph to make the point bigger. Understanding the death of Jesus—a criminal's execution—is central to grasping what he was about. You can see this from the way the four biographers of Jesus devoted a quarter of their pages to the final week of his life. During which time he was arrested, tried, condemned, and executed.

Instead of trying to divert attention from such a dishonorable end the writers seem to do all they can to draw attention to it.

But why? What was it about the death of Jesus that his followers wanted so much to keep in mind?

Why Do People Think He Died?

There are many opinions about Jesus and his death. I've had said to me things like

- Jesus died because people could not live with the truth he taught.
- Jesus was a revolutionary and got caught up in a plot to overthrow the Romans who were oppressing his people.
- Jesus was a wimp and as such was an easy target for the Romans to make an example of.
- Jesus was the victim of the greed of someone who betrayed him for money.

How tragic if any of these were true. Because—in every instance— Jesus would have died caught off-guard and misunderstood, having failed to achieve what he wanted. A life so full of promise would have ended in defeat and even disgrace.

What Was His Crime?

Are any of these theories on the mark? Or are they all wrong? What was the real reason for the death of Jesus? After all, if he was such a good and kind person, why was he strung up like a common criminal? What crime could they lay at his door?

In the eyes of the Jewish religious leaders

So far as the Jewish leaders of the day were concerned, Jesus had committed the greatest crime in the book—to say he was both God and
man by his words and his actions. He actually said both by his words
and his actions.

His popularity didn't go down too well with them either.
Enormous crowds flocked to see and hear him—sometimes ten
thousand or more. He also had an aggravating habit of undermin-
ing their authority by flouting the picky rules they had accumulated down through the years—by doing things like healing people
on the Sabbath, the Jewish holy day.

Then he added cream and sugar by telling them they were hypocrites. But ultimately, it was Jesus declaring himself as God that stuck
in their throats.

In the eyes of the Roman authorities

The Romans were in control of Israel at the time, which meant the
Jewish authorities had no power to punish Jesus themselves. For that,
they had to turn to the Romans.

So, with the end justifying the means, Jewish leaders came up with
a few more charges and some lying witnesses. Which is why Jesus
found himself tried for a Jewish crime by a Roman court.

And, the governor, Pontius Pilate, sentenced him to death because
of his own complacency and for the sake of peace and quiet—even
though his own verdict was, "I find no basis for a charge against this
man."[25]

What Jesus said about his death

In a remarkable way, Jesus had a very clear understanding about what
was on the horizon for him and why it would happen.

It did not take him by surprise. Like a person told by the doctor, "I'm
sorry, you have only six months to live," Jesus knew his death was coming and even what form it would take.

He was clear enough to be able to tell his close friends and followers that the authorities were going to kill him.[26] He even told them how

he would die when he said to his followers, "when I am lifted up from the earth I will draw all people to myself."[27]

It was for a specific purpose. Not only did Jesus know he would die, he knew why. He spoke of his death not being aimless, or down to misfortune, or as simply an occupational hazard. There was a specific intention behind it.

He told his followers, "The reason I came to Earth is so I can give my life as a ransom for many people."[28] What that means we will come to in a moment. For now, it's enough to see that his death was not a random event, but—by his assessment—something Jesus specifically came to do.

What Jesus Did About His Death

Jesus did nothing to stop the process that led to his death. He went willingly to face his executioners. No top legal team was summoned to his defense. No ducking and diving or taking the Fifth Amendment. No "It depends what you mean by 'God'" stuff to escape the charge of blasphemy. Instead

- He told his followers, "No one takes my life from me, but I willingly lay it down . . ."[29]
- He said that he could have called on angelic troops to rescue him, but he chose not to.[30]
- He silently soaked up blows and abuse from people, priests, and soldiers.[31]
- When asked by the Roman governor Pilate to defend himself, Jesus remained silent—in spite of knowing that only Pilate could grant his freedom.[32]

The Gospel writers go so far as to tell us that, at the time of his death, "he gave up his spirit."[33] Jesus even decided the exact time he would release his spirit from his body. It was only to be at the moment when all that his death was intended to achieve had been accomplished.

The Identity of Jesus Is the Key

So Jesus was accused by Jewish leaders, prosecuted by a Roman governor, and Roman soldiers literally nailed him to a cross. But who killed

him? The answer is "I did"—and so did you. Such a provocative statement can only make sense when we fully understand who Jesus was.

God's love in action

The significance of Jesus' death is ultimately all wrapped up in who he
was and what he came to do.

Jesus didn't stumble onto the stage of history. The script had already
been written—with him as the central character. He was to be the king-
pin of God's rescue plan. The one who would deliver us all from the consequences of our sin.

For hundreds of years such a deliverer had been promised through
the Jewish scriptures. This was not by way of some "Mystic Meg,"
fortune-telling, shot-in-the-dark predictions, but through clear statements recorded in the Bible centuries before Jesus was ever born.

These prophecies included specific details about the one who would
come as the deliverer, such as

- He would be born in Bethlehem[34]
- Of a virgin[35]
- He would be betrayed by a friend[36]
- And sold for thirty pieces of silver[37]
- He would be struck and spat on[38]
- While his hands and feet would be pierced[39]
- And so would his side[40]
- The soldiers would throw dice for his clothes[41]
- While never breaking a bone of his body[42]
- He would be buried in a rich man's grave[43]
- And would rise again from the dead.[44]

Do you know what the odds would be for any one person fulfilling even
any eight of the eleven prophecies listed above? It would be like hir-
ing the largest stadium in the world and filling it to overflowing with
rice. Then getting one of those fancy rice-writers—the ones you see on
the streets of major cities around the world (you know, the ones who
can write your name on a grain of rice)—to write YOUR name on a
grain of rice. Then have your precious self-named-fancy-rice-grain
dropped and mixed into the stadium full of rice. Finally, have yourself
blindfolded and reach in and grab your fancy rice grain on your first

try. That's how easy it is—and thus how clear it is that Jesus was THE one.

Don't imagine that Jesus was just a sharp operator who maneuvered things so these prophecies worked out for him, becoming a hero of history through his own cunning. To do that he would have to control where he was born and how he would die, stop his executioners breaking his bones while they broke those of the men dying with him, arrange for his followers to select his grave after he had died, and then raise himself from the dead.

What Was the Point of Jesus' Death?

To understand what the death of Jesus meant involves understanding the picture of sacrifice, which had deep meaning for the Jewish people.

I realize our modern minds may be unnerved at the thought of animal sacrifice. If you feel that way, don't ever ask someone in the poultry business how that poor defenceless chicken ended up as a clean shrink-wrapped carcass ready for you to drop into your food shopping basket.

The picture of sacrifice

At the time when Jesus was first beginning to teach and heal, his cousin John the Baptist pointed to him and said, "Look, the Lamb of God, who takes away the sin of the world!"[45]

The Jewish people listening knew exactly what John was getting at. Their religion was a sacrificial one. They sacrificed animals to show God their willingness to turn away from the wrongs they had done and make a fresh start with him. Let me explain how it worked.

The person who needed forgiveness would bring an animal without any defects to the priest. This was to die as a substitute for them. First their hands were placed on the animal's head as an act of transfer. The blamelessness of the animal was then understood to have been exchanged for their guilt.

With the penalty for sin being death—the animal's throat was then slit. And when it died it carried the sin away with it. Justice had been satisfied.

Here was a graphic picture of a life for a life. The innocent was slain so the guilty could go free. Which was exactly what John the Baptist said Jesus came to do. Jesus was to be the Lamb, sacrificed for the sin of the whole world.

And that was what happened on the cross when Jesus died.

Jesus Was God's Once-For-All-Time Sacrifice

Sacrifice—with an animal, a priest, a knife, and a sinner—was needed regularly to keep paying sin's price.

But Jesus' death was once and for always. When Jesus cried from the cross, "It is finished,"[46] it was. The God of the cosmos did what no animal sacrifice could ever do. He paid the price for the sin—and rescue—of the whole world. He fully and finally made one sacrifice—there on the cross.

This is the ransom I mentioned earlier. Jesus said, "I have come to give my life as a ransom for many."[47] It's as simple as that. Sin has kidnapped us at gunpoint and left the ransom note: "If you want to be rescued, give me more money than you can ever get your hands on—that is, if you want your life back!"

"That's impossible!" you protest.

"I know," says sin with a smirk. And that's the problem.

The Day the Sun Stopped Shining

I'd like to help you grasp the immensity of the price Jesus paid to make our forgiveness and rescue possible. Picture the scene. You're there on that momentous day looking up at the cross. It's noon. Suddenly you can't even see Jesus. You can barely even make out the face of the person next to you. In the middle of the day it's gone as black as midnight.

Don't be surprised. More than eight hundred years before this incredible event a prophet named Amos predicted such a unique day in the future. He wrote, "'In that day,' declares the Sovereign LORD, 'I will make the sun go down at noon and make the earth dark in broad daylight.' "[48]

As you stand there, the day foretold by Amos has finally come. What you are seeing will be written up by Luke in his gospel, saying, "It was now about the sixth hour [12 noon], and darkness came over the whole land until the ninth hour [3 p.m.], for the sun stopped shining. . . ."[49]

The darkness showed God's curse

That darkness points to the magnitude of what is taking place. Despite all that Jesus physically suffered, there was a far greater pain in the heart of God. It was so deep and mysterious that no human eye could see, or mind imagine, what it was that Jesus was suffering.

As you stand and watch, God's judgment for sin—our sin—is being poured out on Jesus. It's just as the prophet Isaiah foretold when he wrote, "he was pierced for our transgressions, he was crushed for our iniquities; the punishment that brought us peace was upon him, and by his wounds we are healed."[50]

Just like a sacrificial lamb—in the darkness—wave after wave of sin pours upon the sinless Savior, and Jesus becomes the curse of the world. He drowns in our sin on a midnight afternoon.

The darkness showed Jesus was utterly forsaken

Jesus experienced utter abandonment because of our sin. For the very first time in eternity he was separated from the Father. As Jesus cried out, "My God, my God why have you forsaken me?"[51] The God who could not look upon sin could not look upon his Son.

In a way that our human minds will never grasp, the one who had never sinned became sin for us. And God could only turn his face. Father and Son were torn apart. And day became night.

The darkness showed a wound in eternity

In one sense, this was an everlasting night. For a God who lives outside of time, those hours on the cross will last for ever. Those wounds of Jesus will never heal. His love is from everlasting to everlasting.

And he did it all for us—to rescue us from the penalty of our sin and provide for our forgiveness.

A Way to Understand It

What Jesus did for us reminds me of a story I heard involving two brothers.

The younger brother ran with a street gang. One night during a fight the knife in his hand met the soft flesh of a rival. Death was swift. The young man ran home to exchange bloodstained clothes for clean ones and fled back into the night.

The older brother arrived home soon afterwards—to discover the garments on the floor and police sirens wailing. By the time the police arrived he was wearing the discarded bloody apparel as though it were his own.

Eventually the older brother was charged, tried, and executed for first degree murder. During all this his younger brother silently witnessed the love of his older sibling—who died in his place and paid his penalty.

Finally it became more than he could bear. Overcome with remorse, he turned himself in and confessed all. But the police sent him away. There could be no charges because his brother's death had fully satisfied the demands of the law. Justice had been done.

And that, in essence, is exactly what God has done for us. To deal with our sin in a way that is both just and loving, he has taken our punishment onto himself. This is what Jesus came to do and is what makes his death so unique.

Three Ways to Respond

When animals were sacrificed as part of the Jewish religion, there were three ways people responded: the good, the bad, and the ugly.

The "good" response involved the person taking it seriously. Turning their back on their wrongs, they looked forward to a fresh start with God. They genuinely trusted in God's promise that the blame on their shoulders would be placed on the animal.

A "bad" response was one of hypocrisy. A sacrifice would be brought only so they could keep on doing wrong. It was sin on easy payments— the more they did wrong, the more they brought sacrifices.

The "ugly" response came from those who couldn't hack the system at all. They just ignored it. They weren't bothered about a relationship with God, and figured they'd worry about their wrongdoings if and when they saw him.

The same is true today. You can choose the way you respond to what Jesus has done for us.

The good way is to believe. The price for our rescue and forgiveness has been paid. All we have to do is to accept God's forgiveness. Not by just intellectually believing it happened in history but personally claiming Jesus' sacrifice for ourselves.

In this act of faith we actively believe our sin and its consequences have been placed on Jesus—and we are now clean and forgiven.

The bad way is to get religious about it. We can admire the drama, stick rigidly to what Jesus taught, and turn everything into an outward observance—but still fail to make the sacrifice of Jesus personal to us. In this way we are no more than unforgiven admirers.

The ugly way is to reject God's generous offer altogether. How could such a wonderful gift be left neglected and unopened? It's like being caught in a flood, stranded on your rooftop with the water still rising higher—up to your chest—certain death is near. Then suddenly a rescue-copter comes and drops a ladder for your recovery. But you wave the help away with the words, "I can save myself," while the water now gathers around your neck.

It's beyond me why someone would reject God's offer for help. It means the penalty for our sin remains unpaid—until we ourselves pay its terrible price.

The Difference that Waits

If you accept God's hand of help—if you accept the sacrifice Jesus made as counting for yourself—so much becomes yours.

A clean slate. The payment you owed has been wiped off the books. You are debt free.

And God does something we can't. Ever been told by a friend, "Forget I told you that"? It's impossible. But God can choose to forget. He puts our sin behind his back and decides never to think of it again.

A clear conscience. There is nothing left for you to feel guilty about. The past is gone. The heavenly delete button has been pressed. The record of your wrongdoings and the penalty due has vanished. There are no back-up copies to haunt you.

A restored relationship. God now sees you as though you had never sinned—because you have been forgiven. So you can now feel clean and comfortable in his presence.

By getting this far you have already made quite a journey. But could there still be some big doubts in the way—in the form of some tough and nagging questions? Well, stick with me because the next few chapters face up to some of the most likely—and the most difficult.

WAY TO GO

Can God be reached by any road you travel?

You'll have noticed by now that this book is not just about filling your head with new ideas. I'm after your life. You suspected as much? I thought so.

These pages aim to do far more than help you win the right colored slice of pie next time a question about religion crops up in a game of "Trivial Pursuit." Nor will they land you with the grand prize in a round of *Who Wants to be a Millionaire*.

Everything I'm giving you is more than that. It's information for action. In the end you're going to have to decide whether or not to jump. This will mean either saying, "Thanks, but no thanks." Or actively saying "Yes" to Jesus and all he stands for.

Right now, the thought of giving Jesus a hearty cry of "Yeah! Gimme all you got" may seem as possible as all those plane-crash survivors in *Lost* finding their way off the island. There are probably a few heavy-duty questions lurking at the back of your battered mind and you may wonder if such a decision involves kissing your intellect goodbye.

As we journey up the craggy path of "things to get straight before following Jesus," there are a few giant boulders standing in the way of your progress. These huge rocks are the big questions you need answers to. And it just wouldn't be fair to take you this far up the road only to drop you with a pat on the head and a "Have a nice life!"

That's why the next few chapters hit full on some of the biggest questions asked when people are weighing up the odds about becoming followers of Jesus. Big questions like "Other religions," "Suffering," "Life after death," "What is faith?" and "If I say yes, can I really make it stick?" I'm not saying you will end up with everything nailed down. But let's take an intelligent look. You deserve it.

How Can One Religion Be Right Out of So Many?

For a start, where do all the other religions in the world fit in? After all, most people know a deeply religious person—or three—where Jesus is nowhere part of the picture. Perhaps they are neighbors or friends or your doctor, or they run your local Indian restaurant. And, in each case, they are just one of millions around the world who believe what they do.

And you're questioning whether it's reasonable to accept that these sincere, friendly, and helpful people can be wrong. Or are they as right as anyone else, because all religions are much the same anyway? Does it even matter? And if it does, how can anyone possibly know which to choose out of such a rich assortment?

Come with me on a journey through the supermarket of faith to see if we can find some answers.

Where we can agree

Wherever we turn in our now global world we can't help but fall over the impact made by other faiths and cultures. Whether it's different kinds of food, the varying choice of music, the many types of movies on offer, or the multiple ways of thinking and approaching the situations life throws at us. In fact, we all experience a richer, fuller life because of the impact of those from various faiths and backgrounds.

Sadly, with religion and conflict now so strongly linked together there is the danger of stereotypes—where the worst we see flashed before us in the news is what we base our opinions of other religions on.

But followers of every religion can be easily and unfairly stereotyped. Faithful Muslims will quickly—and rightly—distance themselves from the suicide bombers of 9/11. Just like faithful Catholics will distance themselves from the Irish Republican terrorists of yesteryear.

Just because your local "Wok-A-Thon" Chinese restaurant was caught with rats swimming in the soup is no reason to judge every chop suey house on the same basis. But we do that so often when it comes to other religions.

As a result we forget too easily that the major faiths around the globe—and some minor ones too—have made very significant contributions to our lives and our culture.

For example:

They have added cultural richness. Our planet is a more varied and interesting place to live because of them. Take the beauty of Muslim art and architecture, the haunting strains of Hindu music, or the liveliness of Jewish feasts and celebrations, for example.

These, and so many other traditions, have broadened our appreciation of what it means to be alive, express ourselves, and relate to others.

They uphold strong moral values. In many ways the world faiths have been custodians of the values that have kept society from drifting into chaos. These values have been the basis for the principles of law and order that help maintain justice.

Religions also guide us toward being better people by instructing us to care for the poor, the old, and the weak—as well as the living environment. No religion offers easy or cheap short-cuts to goodness or success—they are all morally demanding.

They do their best to make sense of the world. All religions point to the fact that human beings are not the center of the universe. And that there is some reality outside of human life that can make sense of our existence.

They also agree that death is something we must take account of and include in how we view this life.

Are All Religions Much the Same?

But are the major religions of the world much like ketchup? There's a rumor—denied vigorously by Heinz—that there's only one ketchup factory in the known universe. And no matter what brand is on the bottle, we all eat the same stuff.

True or not, is that how it is with religions? The label may read Buddhism, Islam, Christianity, Hinduism or whatever—but is the substance inside any different? Do they all worship the same God and have the same nutritional content?

The more you know about ketchup the more convinced you will be that the "one factory" theory is wide of the mark. The same applies to religion. Those who know little on the subject may assume only the packaging is different. But it's certainly not a view anyone on the inside of any religion holds. Because they know how starkly different their beliefs are from each other.

What kind of God?

Take the issue of God for example. The major world religions all believe quite different things.

- A Hindu will tell you there are countless gods—who all work to their own set of rules.
- Buddhists don't speak about God or whether he even exists.
- A Muslim will explain that there is only one God but he is unknowable.
- A Christian believes there is only one God and he can be known intimately and personally.

Is it really possible for God to be an impersonal and unknowable force in one religion—and to be an intimate and knowable Creator in another? How can God be Lord of the whole universe for one faith and for another be one of thousands of deities to be worshipped?

How to keep God on your side

Let's look at it another way. How do the major religions believe you go about staying in God's good books?

- A Muslim will tell you it's by observing a regular system of prayer, fasting, and by giving to the poor.
- A Hindu will tell you it's a matter of appeasing the many gods by worshipping at a shrine or an idol, and practicing personal discipline.
- A Buddhist believes there is no God to keep in with—but that by looking inward and doing good you will get a better deal next time round.
- A Christian will tell you it's by personally trusting in Jesus as his follower.

These religions are not even expressing complementary views which go together to form a complete picture. It's not like a diverse group of people describing a new car, with some talking about its performance, others about its engineering, and still others about its color and style.

The views of other faiths are not complementary but actually contradictory. The car's red. No, blue. It's powered by diesel. No, an electric battery. It's got an 18-foot wheel base, six doors, a cocktail cabinet, and two fluffy dice on the back shelf. No, it's a two-door Mini with "Gorgeous George" and a monkey face emblazoned on the sides.

They are that different. Which leads to a very heavy question . . . They may be very different, but do all religions lead to God anyway?

The Problem: God Is Not a City

Is it true, as some have been heard to say, that God is like a city and all roads lead to him? It sure is a sweet concept. Very charming. Let's just think through this attractive thought.

If God were a city we could approach him by any number of routes. We could take "Muslim Avenue" or "Hindu Street." We could take the "Christian Boulevard." Or maybe one of the minor roads we pave ourselves. So many options. Which way should I go to reach my final destination? Perhaps I could do a bit of all of them if I pick the route with care.

But God is not a city—God is a person. If he were a city we could approach him on any given road. And from the air and by tunnels. But God is not a destination to be reached—he is a person. And as a person, just like you and me, he is reached only through a relationship—and on his terms.

God has feelings, views, expectations, likes, and dislikes—and relates to us on that basis. A city has character, not personality. So while the city limit sign may say "Welcome" it doesn't have a heart that leaps for joy when you get there.

Isn't Sincerity Enough?

If we are to claim that "all religions lead to God" we had better be able to define "all." So here come some questions.

First, what qualifies a religion to get you to God? Do all religions count no matter their size? Like the one with six members, including a goldfish, that meet at a bus stop on alternate Wednesdays? Or is it only bigger religions—in which case, how much bigger do you have to be? Is 500 the pass mark? Or less? Or more? And who decides?

Or is it only the big five or so? Do they have a monopoly on heaven in the same way the oil companies are working to have a monopoly on transportation?

But if size is not the issue is it okay to include religions no matter what they believe? What about those that worship trees, sacrifice their young or are convinced that we are descended from Ming and Mong—two turtles from the planet Grebniets?

Though this may all sound a bit daft it is even dafter not to face the issue.

But perhaps what matters most is the need to be sincere—even if it does include bus stops, trees, or the planet Grebniets. Sure, some religions may have got things a bit wrong but isn't it enough to be sincere?

This one's simple. Have you ever been in an argument over something provable? Like how to spell Häagen-Dazs. I strongly disagreed with my friend Joseph over its spelling earlier in the book. I told him, I know how to spell it: H-A-G-E-N—D-A-S!

In the end he went to a shop and bought one—ate it—and then showed me the carton and the correct spelling. What a pig. Not Joseph—but the fact I got it wrong.

The point I'm making is, despite my sincerity, the spelling on the carton did not change to accommodate me. In the same way, we all get it sincerely wrong at times. But so far as religion is concerned, does it matter? If you think it doesn't—and remember it's not how to spell some made-up word that we're talking about—let me ask you a question. How come belief in God is the only big issue in the universe for which sincerity is all that matters?

Next time you fly, do you want a pilot who is cast-iron confident about how to land? Or just one who is sincere? Next time you're under the surgeon's knife, do you want him fully up to date with the latest medical training? Or will a good dollop of sincerity be enough? Next time you hit the road for a six-hour journey, do you plan to have a map handy? Or simply set out overdosed on sincerity?

If you are still on the "sincerity is all that matters" kick, does this mean you admire the sincerity of Adolf Hitler, Joseph Stalin, Osama Bin

Laden, Kim Jong-il, and even our own political leaders? And that God feels the same way?

You get my drift. Right is right and wrong is wrong, no matter how sincere or insincere we are.

What Does Jesus Say About Other Religions?

But never mind my own opinion. Let's turn to someone who has a right to a view—Jesus. What's his verdict on all this? He puts it simply and plainly by saying, "I am the way and the truth and the life. No-one comes to the Father except through me."[52]

Pause and read that again. It's worth it.

And now let's think through what he is saying, step by step.

Jesus said "the way." First he tells us there is a road that gets there. The Father—God—is reachable.

Jesus said "the" way, not "a" way. Second he makes clear that we don't have a variety of possible routes to the end destination. There's not a super-highway, a pretty way along the back lanes, and a few others in between. Not a great way, a not-so-good way, and a "you're-bound-to-get-stuck-behind-some-slow-moving-vehicle" way.

It's like the path between two train stations. There's the train track or there's the train track.

Jesus said "the way" and "the truth" go together. He makes no mention of sincerity or best guesses. Rather, he links the journey to be made with one of truth.

Please allow me to be technical for a moment. Jesus didn't speak English. And the word he used that has been translated "truth" is not truth in terms of "a fact that is accurate." It's a word that would be used to describe the "real thing."

Without doubt, you have bought a cheap copy of a designer label garment. What you had was not authentic—and you eventually noticed the difference. It had all the style and swagger of the real thing—on the outside. Then came the test—the first time you washed it. Remember the result? You're probably still using it to clean the car.

Jesus was saying "the way" has to do with him being the real thing. The authentic one.

Jesus said "No one." By that he meant "no one." Or to put it another way, "no one." And, if you check out the words he used that we have translated as "no one," you will find they mean—wait for it—"no one." By now you have probably got the picture.

What Makes Jesus So Different?

What lies at the heart of Jesus' astonishing claim is the stark contrast between him and every other religious leader or founder of a religion. Jesus is uniquely the way because he alone deals with the three greatest issues of life.

He pays our debt

All the other religions of the world demand their followers do something to work their way into God's good books. They may each propose different things but the message is the same—do enough and get it right and you'll be okay . . . maybe.

It's the religious version of the reward schemes many stores now offer. The ones where you spend half of what you earn in return for enough reward points to buy a pack of gum and a roll of toilet paper. That's what earning points is like the world over. And that's what the religions of the world expect you to do. Some people even wrongly think this is what Jesus expects. That it's all down to earning points with God—redeemable tokens for the end of time.

In their mind they expect, one day, to stand in line at the gates of heaven where a celestial checkout girl says, "Okay, so let's weigh up all the bad things you've done. Hmmmm. And can I have your tokens, please? That's quite a stack there—let me count 'em up. Oh dear. What a shame you didn't clock it when you had that heart attack a few years back. You were in credit then. But now you're four tokens short."

God isn't like that. He doesn't enslave us to the eternal "weights and balances," so that we're for ever trying to make up for the wrong things we have done. And never knowing whether or not we've done enough.

While this is the treadmill other religions put people on, Jesus offers something completely different. When it comes to the eternal check-out counter—the register is closed and the way is wide open—because Jesus is *the way*.

While all other religions ask their followers to earn points to claim the prize that can never be earned—Jesus is the free gift of life to any who will receive him.

He gives us the strength we need

While other religions tell us how to live, Jesus gives us the power to live. The full details come in a later chapter but let me just touch on the principles.

The problem with religion is it can never change a person's heart. But Jesus can. What he offers is not only forgiveness and a new start, but also a whole new operating system. Or, to put it in terms of what a decayed house needs—a complete rewiring.

That's not a perfect illustration. But it gets to the heart of the issue. When we put our faith in all that Jesus did—and commit our lives to him—God does the same for us as he did for Jesus. He raises us from the dead—spiritually. We actually become "alive to God"[53] in a way we never were before.

He provides a dynamic relationship

The other thing Jesus offers that no religion does is a living relationship with God himself. I can't be friends with a law or a creed or a dogma. But only with a person.

We are not left to treat God like a set of rules to be broken and then pieced back together again. God is not law—he is alive. He's a living person—someone who longs to know us.

Is it any wonder Jesus is the only way, when he alone offers

- The certainty of forgiveness—through his death on the cross
- A new spiritual life—through his power in us
- A new relationship—through his personal companionship.

What a way to go!

What Happens to Those Who Sincerely Get it Wrong?

If all the above is true we still have to face a very awkward question. Would a loving God really thumb his nose at good people who climbed the wrong tree in their sincere search to find him? Would he really lock them out of his presence because they never heard or understood the good news about Jesus?

My honest answer is, I don't know how God will deal with those jungle tribesfolk from the back of beyond, or my Muslim friends who run the local grocery store. Or what his plans are for my accountant who follows an ancient religion from the East. And I don't need to know. Issues like that are best left to God himself.

What I do know is, whatever happens, God will be absolutely fair about it. And such is his character that he will be looking for reasons to get people into heaven rather than for excuses to keep them out.

But I also know, if there were some other way for sin to be forgiven other than through the sacrifice of his Son, God would have taken it.

I do know that, however it ends up, these people I so love and respect are missing out on the exhilarating joy of going through life with a clear conscience and the close companionship of the God who made them.

Finally, having faced a barrage of your questions, allow me one of my own. If there is a way to reach God, have you taken it?

Now, with one big boulder blocking the road to belief out of the way, here comes another—and it's the question more often asked than any other.

10 WHAT A PAIN

Isn't there just too much suffering to believe?

When it comes to life's big questions, there's one that dwarfs all of the other great mysteries—even brain-stretchers like "How do you know when it's time to tune your bagpipes?"

This big question, to put it simply, is "If God is so good, loving, and powerful, why doesn't he stop all the suffering?"

The World Is in Pain

Almost every day horrendous images flash across our TV screens. Stark pictures—of weeping children, distraught mothers, or devastated communities. The cause may be an earthquake or a tyrant, a famine or a terrorist, or some other cause of human suffering. But the outcome is still the same—pain, together with the anguished cry, "Why, God, why?!?!"

And the pain is not all "out there." Just running through the names in my own address list brings an ache. There are the friends whose first child died within days of its birth. Another whose wife has almost wasted away from multiple sclerosis. Another whose cherished first child will never walk.

So is God a cosmic sadist who rejoices over inflicting pain on creatures who can't fight back? Is he no better than a spiteful child pulling the wings off butterflies for sport? Or is he a bumbling, ineffectual designer? Is this world, as Van Gogh put it, "one of his sketches that turned out badly"?

Can We Possibly Make Sense of it All?

It is here I need to be transparently honest. If there were one clear and simple answer to why God lets people suffer you could bottle it and make a fortune.

There is no easy, done-and-dusted, answer waiting in the wings. Instead it's a bit like putting together a jigsaw puzzle—hopefully not as bad as the 1,000-piece picture of writhing earthworms. Even then we may have to cope with a few of the pieces being missing.

But this is too big a question to dodge and it deserves at least my best shot.

Is God the Only One to Blame?

For a start, how fair is it to blame God for so much that has nothing to do with him in the first place?

Did God plant all the landmines now randomly blowing legs off innocent children? Was he personally responsible for the inefficient management of the Union Carbide factory in Bhopal, India, where lethal gas leaks killed over fifteen thousand and poisoned countless more? Did he start Rwanda's intertribal genocide that massacred 80,000 and created a generation of orphans?

More than that, it is hardly God's fault that so much human suffering is allowed to continue. The world spends $780 billion a year on the military. Yet a mere $8 billion would help the world feed itself, so ending hunger; $9 billion would give the world clean and safe water to drink. And $6 billion could give every child a sound primary education.

There are even things "we" do that contribute to the impact of natural disasters. For example, the knowledge exists on how to construct buildings that can withstand an earthquake. We know how to give an early warning of a tsunami. We know what we are doing to generate global warming and the impact this will have. But often, for economic reasons, we don't put this knowledge to work. And needless suffering is the outcome.

Come to that, millions of us—yes, I'm in on this—fail to eat our veggies, fight the flab, or control what reaches our intestines to the degree that the health that ought to be ours isn't.

But this is only part of the story. After all, we are not to blame for everything bad happening in our world—which puts God right in the firing line.

The Way Things Are Is Not Plan A

Given the chance to defend himself, I think the first thing God would say is, "This is not the way things were intended to be."

The opening pages of the Bible paint a vivid picture of humanity in a beautiful garden in the midst of the whole of creation. As God surveyed the work of his hands he declared everything to be "good." And that's not "good" as in "nice" or "okay." But "good" as in "absolutely mind-blowingly perfect"—and then some.

That is the way God made things and intended them to be—for ever. Plan A.

In such a world, nature would never misbehave and people would live the same way—with no grab and greed, no might is right, no me at the expense of you.

That's a vivid picture of the way this God we have been exploring intended our world to be. With everything in creation at peace with itself and with everything else.

What went wrong was that the humans chose to do it their way. The opportunity for them to behave as though they were God had been placed off-limits. But they decided to willfully disobey and trespass.

At that moment rebellion came into the world. What happened next was like the gears of a car being crunched into reverse while speeding forward down an open highway. With a heart-tearing lurch, the whole of creation shook and splintered—never again to run as it was meant to.

For those who caused this catastrophe, there was no longer a place in the garden. Their relationship with the Creator was shattered. They now felt exposed and naked. And everything had been spoilt. From top to bottom and middle to outside. The "good" became "ugly." Everything became spoilt—from human behavior to the balance of the environment. And it has remained that way ever since.

Sickness and pain were not in the original script but now they are here.

Our blunderful world is all down to us. And the key word is "sin." Because that's what caused the mess and continues to do so.

We've Been Given the Dignity of Choice

Even so, couldn't God step in to stop all the pain and suffering? Isn't that what a "loving God" would do? After all, if you see a child with a sharp object you take it away. If they are heading down the street you hold their hand. If a truck is about to mow them down you snatch them to safety. Why doesn't God do the same?

As the Creator of everything, God could do exactly that. But by him doing so we'd never be free to make our own decisions, never have the dignity of growing to maturity. That wouldn't be a life—that would be a puppet show.

God could program people never to make mistakes or behave badly. But do you want to live on a whole planet full of android types like "Data" from *Star Trek*? What bliss! What perfection! "I'm sorry sir, I just can't help being good and serving others all the time. It's all I'm programmed to do!" We would have no wars—not even two people having a disagreement. But people would not be human. And, as you would be one of them, neither would you.

God is powerful enough to remove all evil from the Earth, if that's the way he wanted to play it. But would you want it? Do you fancy living in a place like Seahaven, the TV-location-city featured in the Jim Carrey film *The Truman Show*? This controlled environment was populated by people pushing baby carriages, riding bicycles, and cleaning their spotless houses in exactly the same way every day for all of time. And all presided over by the watchful benevolent producer—God.

For everyone in Seahaven, except Truman, this was adequate—because they were actors. But Truman wasn't scripted by the cosmic producer. He was a real, living human with needs and desires and frustrations, which eventually made him yearn to break out of the perfect world.

We can't have it both ways. Either we will be in Seahaven performing to someone else's script, or on a planet where we are allowed the dignity of choice. And once we get to choose, sometimes we will choose harm—to ourselves and to others.

God could snuff out anyone who may cause suffering to another. Great idea—and we all have our own list of where he should start. High on the "snuff" list would be the big baddies like terrorists and tyrants and my neighbors with the dog. But to eradicate all pain we couldn't stop there.

The axe would have to fall on all who had or could—intentionally or accidentally—cause anyone to suffer.

Do you know what that means? We'd all be on the "snuff" list. Not very high up, maybe. But, according to your view of the way things should be, soon God would have to come knocking on your door and mine. No one would escape because human nature has been less than perfect since that great grinding of gears.

Even so, you may still be saying, "I don't understand." But what if there is no way we could ever understand?

Our Understanding Is Limited

Suppose there are answers to the huge questions surrounding God and suffering but they are beyond our ability to grasp. And even if God *did* sit down with us over a cup of coffee to explain it all, he would have to use vocabulary we never learned and mathematical formulas we could never comprehend. Suppose the answers that God wants to provide are way beyond our ability to understand?

Of all the traumas to have befallen my children, the one that haunts me the most concerns my third son, Aran, when he was about four years old. Running across our backyard at frenetic speed, he tripped. Head and bench collided, badly tearing the corner of Aran's eyelid.

The necessary stitches required a local anesthetic, but the injection did not allow him to look the other way. The result was an agonizing ten minutes while I physically held down the son I loved for the essential treatment to take place.

There, wrapped in my arms and doggedly fighting, Aran's very best interests were being served. But, from his fearful and confused perspective, I was contributing to his pain. All he could say was, "Daddy," as we both cried together. And by that he meant, "Daddy, why?" I longed to explain. But there was no way he could understand.

Think of it this way: every normal child reaches the "Why?" stage. Why this? Why that? What's it for? What does it do? How does it work? Why? Why? Why? And time and again the adult on the receiving end of the barrage has the answer to hand—but the child's vocabulary, intellect, and experience deny it the capacity to understand the answer.

Could that be how it is on some of the issues of suffering? That God would love to let us in on the answers but we don't have the capacity to deal with them?

Is All "Bad" Really "Bad"?

There's also something else we should wrap our minds round. It doesn't close the book on the issue but it adds a deeper perspective. It's the thought that not everything we see as "bad" truly is "bad" when it comes to the grand scale of things.

I don't want to trivialize the suffering of millions or of any individual. But allow me to draw on my own experience, along with that of Rosemary, my wife. Our family trudged through some long dark days with her cancer and then several years of a deep depressive illness. Yet because of all we went through we now see ourselves as far richer and more complete people. Strange to say but we wouldn't have wanted to miss it.

What I'm driving at is that millions of people, including Rosemary and me, are richer and more complete as the result of the pain and suffering that exists in the world. Indeed, what a shallow existence we would be consigned to without adversity to overcome, opportunities for the human spirit to soar, the means for people to become truly rich on the inside through triumphing against all the odds.

No, I'm not saying that wars, earthquakes, sickness, and the like are "good." I'm saying that we should not be blind to the positive impact suffering can have. I've seen it personally in some of the world's poorest communities and in the lives of those closest to me.

Let's face it, the most valuable and genuinely likeable people are quite often those who have suffered. And the most bland and empty are usually those who have sailed through life unscathed. Which suggests there might be more to living and growing old with pain and hardship than to do so in absolute comfort and perpetual sunshine. And God knows this too.

Seeing the Bigger Picture

Finally, if we want God to give account of the bad that's here, it is only fair to insist he gets "blamed" for the good. We need to see the whole canvas and not just the seemingly grotesque black area that is part of it.

On that canvas, do we see all the bravery and self-sacrifice seen in response to 9/11? Or the outpouring of passionate and sacrificial response to the tsunami that hit the South Asian coast a few Christmases ago? And those amazing acts of generosity and self-sacrifice that happen every hour of the day on every square mile of the globe? Let's be sure to blame God for all this and everything like it.

On that canvas too, God has painted his love for us in the richest of colors. He has committed the most lavishly outrageous act of self-sacrifice that can be imagined.

The God who stands accused of indifference to our pain actually loves his creation so much he was willing to cause himself the greatest pain ever endured—because that's what happened when he sent Jesus. Far from enjoying the spectacle of us suffering, he entered our world and suffered with us.

Any attempt to make sense of pain and suffering has to deal with what we know about God just as much as what we know about suffering. And what we know is that he loves us—with extravagant abundance.

There's a story told—I don't know where it originally came from—of the time when God came to judge all the people who ever lived. Most shrank back from the brilliant light before them. But some groups stood their ground.

"What does God know of all that the human race had been forced to endure?" they argued. "God leads a pretty sheltered life." And they decided that before God could be qualified to be their judge, he must endure what they endured. God should be sentenced to live on Earth— as a man!

"Let him be born a Jew. Let people think him illegitimate. Let him live in a country occupied and ruled by a cruel, callous government. Let him be betrayed by his closest friends. Let him face false charges, be tried by a prejudiced jury and convicted by a cowardly judge. Let him be beaten and tortured. At the last, let him see what it means to be terribly alone.

"Then let him die."

When the sentence had been pronounced there was a long silence. No one uttered a word. No one moved. For suddenly all knew that God had already served his sentence.[54]

Far from being removed and remote from this world of pain, God has chosen to grasp it firmly to his heart. And with that thought in mind, let me take you back again to my son Aran and his eye.

As I held his squirming frame while the emergency staff stitched his eye, I gained a clearer perspective of how God must feel.

Here was I, a loving father, moved to tears by the pain of the one held in my embrace. In that moment it came to me—that, in the same way I held my son, God wants us to be fully engulfed in his loving embrace.

In fact, if we could see pain and suffering from God's perspective, perhaps we might even discover that we are not the only ones crying. His eyes are also wet with tears.

# JUST DESSERTS

Is there more to life than what happens on Earth?

According to the very latest statistics, the current death rate stands at 100 percent. Feel free to look at the small print of your "Right to be a Human on the planet Earth" contract—but you'll find the "Life Termination" section has no get-out clause.

Everyone will one day breathe their last. When I go I want to die peacefully in my sleep—like my grandfather did. Not screaming like the passengers in his car. And how can anyone write about death without including the famous Woody Allen quote—"I'm not afraid to die. It's just that I don't want to be there when it happens."

But we will be there—and what then?

What Happens When We Die?

Beliefs on the "After death, what then?" front seem to fall into three basic categories.

Category 1: The big snuff. Some believe death is simply *El Finito*—the end. That at the moment the body quits breathing and the brain stops flickering you are as dead as mutton. It's goodbye and goodnight—with no wake-up call—ever.

They sincerely believe the best you can hope for is that life will be nice while it lasts. But this is all you're going to get.

Category 2: One more time. Cosmic recycling is at the heart of this belief. Far from being the end, this life is just one stepping stone in an ongoing metamorphosis. Depending on how well you did last time, you'll come back as someone—or something—else.

The concept is that our soul will live a succession of lives. In each we are born, live, and die—and then come back to do it all over again. As a cockroach or a king. Or something in between.

Category 3: Heaven, here I come. This is a belief that there's an existence we can consciously experience after death. Different cultures call it different things—Heaven, Nirvana, Elysium, the Happy Hunting Ground, and so on.

Through the centuries people have been buried with their belongings in the belief that they'll need them in their next destination. The Egyptian rulers did it in style. In other cultures, the dead man's wife was thrown on the funeral pyre with him—added to his baggage allowance—in the assumption he would need her in the future.

How Can We Know?

Some argue we can't know anything about a possible afterlife until we get there—or don't, as the case may be. All we can do, they claim, is to hope for the best. But there are reasons to believe we can do better than that. A whole lot better. So let me suggest some.

Our mind tells us. Apart from the emotional tugs of wishing to believe there is something beyond this life, there is also a logic to it. Can you imagine trying to convince an unborn baby that life in the womb was all there was going to be? But why have I got arms? Why have I got legs? What am I supposed to do with them? There must be something more?

What are we meant to do with the knowledge we are assimilating, the character we are building and the spiritual dimension we are developing? Is it really to be put to no good use? Is the womb of this world all there is?

We feel it deep inside. There seems to be so much more than wishful thinking when it comes to believing that beyond all this is something greater and "different."

Throughout the ages there has been a deep-seated belief—a kind of "given"—across all civilizations and cultures that there is another reality outside and beyond us that we join from the moment of death.

Experience supports it. The near-death experience—or NDE—is an encounter no self-respecting cardiac arrest victim seems able to avoid these days.

We have all heard stories of someone "dying" on the operating slab, to find themselves wafting along a long dark tunnel toward a bright light, before being ushered into a world of great beauty. Then a voice tells them, "It's not your time to die—you have to go back." Occasionally the voice adds, "And save the world."

Of course, though the NDE phenomenon is well documented it's nigh impossible to scientifically verify. And claims that such experiences can be down to medication or brain activity under extreme stress have to be heard. Yet it is all too easy to dismiss the evidence purely because there is no test tube involved.

After all, what are we to make of one of the most bizarre aspects of NDEs—when those blind from birth "come back." Although never having sight before, they are able to describe the room they died in—right down to the very last detail.

Until recently, most reported NDEs were warm and fuzzy. But other experiences are now surfacing. For some, NDEs are far from blissful. Instead of a feeling of floating upwards, they report being pulled downwards—toward a pit inhabited by evil beings. A newspaper article a little while back commented on the strange parallels between NDE reports and traditional views of heaven . . . and of hell.

But we are going to need a lot more than NDE accounts—which are possibly nothing more than stress-induced experiences—to convince us as to what happens in the afterlife. We need an expert opinion.

What Did Jesus Say About Life After Death?

The best credentials for speaking about life after death belong to Jesus. After all, human theories and debatable experiences don't hold a match to his firsthand knowledge of death and his authority as God.

Based on Jesus being who he said he was, we can be confident that he has something authentic to say. And he left his hearers in no doubt that there is more to life than what we can see, feel, and touch "down here." So far as life after death is concerned, Jesus made it clear that:

It's a place where he is. To a thief being crucified with him, Jesus said, "I promise that today you will be with me in paradise." So "paradise," which gets to be another word for "heaven," exists and Jesus is there.[55] And note there's nothing here about the thief needing to "go round again" with the chance to do a better job next time. Imperfect though the man was, heaven was to be his very soon indeed.

It's for ever. The picture Jesus used to explain heaven to his followers was of a spacious mansion-style boarding house with many rooms. "I'm going to get things ready for you," he told them.[56]

The reason behind his work, promised Jesus, was because he and his followers would always "be together."[57] That means there is no checkout time, no "passing Go to collect $200," no further hop round the board to do it again. Heaven, says Jesus, is a permanent and ongoing experience.

It's a great place to be. Heaven, says Jesus, is the ideal place to store what you treasure—because there are no thieves, moths or decay.[58] Just think how profound that seemingly simple statement is. "No thieves"—which means in the whole of heaven every single resident will be morally perfect. "No moths"—there will be nothing there to spoil the way things are. "No decay"—everything will stay perfect for ever.

It's a place for those who have pre-registered. Jesus said that heaven's a place where the names of its intended residents are written down before they get there.[59] Those who look to be in heaven also look to have their names on the arrivals list. How do they do it? Like getting into the club on VIP night—its all in who you know and who you trust to get you in when it really matters. Jesus called that pre-registration list the "Book of Life."[60]

Unlike Anything We've Ever Known

These earthly pictures of a heavenly environment help us to wrap our minds round the unknown as best as we are able. But there will always be a limit to what we can grasp because the building fabric of eternity is unlike anything we have ever seen or experienced.

I remember sitting under a tree in a third world village where electricity had yet to arrive. I was trying—and failing—to explain to a family the principles of a washing machine and a dryer. And if you think that's hard, try explaining a laptop computer on a wireless connection to the Internet. When it comes to getting our minds round "heaven" we are like those humble villagers who have never experienced the marvels of electricity. With no experience of the world beyond we cannot even begin to grasp its reality and be blown away by its wonder.

The big travel companies have invested millions to sell the sizzle of faraway places from Mali to Madagascar. But all heaven has had to fight back with have been a few cartoons showing old people on clouds.

I imagine most people have a secret fear that, to anyone other than the Pope, heaven will be as exciting as listening to worms sing. And we will have to do it for ever. And isn't it hard to get your mind round the idea of doing anything—however wonderful—for longer than two or three weeks at a stretch?

But do we really believe the eternal God who created creativity has no more in mind for us than everlasting boredom? As God is there, heaven must surely be the most exhilarating, mind-blowing, ever-changing, always something-up-his-sleeve place. We may not be able to picture it, but if the limited environment of Earth keeps throwing up surprises, the potential of heaven is unimaginable.

Heaven Was Not the Only Place Jesus Spoke About

Please don't overlook exactly who Jesus was speaking to when he said all his stuff about heaven. It wasn't to all and sundry. In every case, the message about heaven and being there with him was to people who were actually following him.

Miss that point and you could assume Jesus wanted us to believe heaven was the place where everyone goes no matter who and what. But that isn't the full picture. Jesus spoke about two separate destinations and a point after death where some people went one way and some the other.

Two Destinations

Jesus explained that after death follows judgment—and he is to be the judge. To help them picture what he meant, the great teacher used an example that his listeners would be really familiar with.

Jesus said it is like separating wheat from chaff. This was an annual event. Every harvest time, as the result of some beating and fanning, the worthless chaff ended up in a different place from the valuable wheat. One went to make food for the hungry. The other went to be burned.[61]

Jesus used this familiar picture to express as simply and plainly as possible the truth that everyone will face judgment following their death. Wheat grew up in the field unimpaired by its inedible equal—chaff. But the day of division and destiny would come.

Our Future Depends on the Issue of Forgiveness

Jesus spoke of judgment as being based not on what wheat or chaff had done—but because of what each was. He didn't speak of good wheat set apart from rebellious chaff. It was their very nature that decided their different destinations.

The wheat-chaff pictures Jesus used were to help us understand the difference between those who "are" and those who "are not." This is because it is essentially "what we are" or "are not" that will impact us in eternity.

But what do we mean by "those who are" and "those who are not"? What is it that determines the judgment we will face? Well, it all comes down to this: Are you forgiven or aren't you? In other words, are you in a relationship with God because you have been freely forgiven by him?

Cabbage stew or shiny suit?

There is a mistaken understanding that many have which makes God into a kind of celestial cabbage seller. They assume God weighs up our good deeds and bad deeds—like cabbages in a market. And if our good outweighs our bad (and most of us assume it does), we get chucked in the "good" basket—fit for the heavenly banquet.

But a much more accurate picture of God is as the eternal tailor. He looks to see what clothes we are wearing. Is it the unforgiven, never-been-washed, so-self-stinky-old-it-sticks-to-your-skin outfit we have insisted on hanging onto? Or the snowdrift white, bleached-clean, so-shiny-new-it-glows-in-the-dark outfit that came as a gift from Jesus along with his forgiveness?

Those who are forgiven will feel comfortable with God and will go to be with him for ever. While those who haven't won't and won't want to.

To be in God's presence, transformed—changed like Cinderella—wearing the new frock of forgiveness, will be a wonderful place to be. Such joy, such an intense sense of belonging and of being where we were always intended to be! But those who stand before him like an ugly sister, with only their wrongdoings to cover them, will suffer an awful shame-filled soul-searing experience.

We Will Be Where We Feel Most at Home

It's not God's fault the wrong we do makes us unwelcome in his presence. It's the result of our choice. Forgiveness is available—through faith in Jesus' death on the cross. But it goes unclaimed.

"Take your umbrella," warned my wife. It was good advice. "I'll be fine," came my reply. And I returned home soaked to the skin. But don't blame the rain. I had a choice.

Eternity is where all that you decided on Earth comes to its fulfillment. If knowing God personally was not an attractive option down here, why should it be any more attractive for eternity?

In the same way, in eternity, God's breath of love will be a fragrant cooling breeze to one person but to another it will be like a burning scorching flame. The light of God's presence will either be sunshine to bathe in—or a million-watt bulb that makes us desperate for cover, like cockroaches blinded by the light.

If your whole life—in all your choices—you have opted for "not God," why at the end of it would you suddenly want to choose him? You will have had all your life to make it clear to God what you want. Why should he disappoint you now? And it would be immoral of him to force on you something you never wanted.

Imagine a magnificent ball in full swing—with everyone dressed up to the hilt. It's that kind of a party. Laughter shakes the walls. The dress code is all fancy gowns and tuxedos. Everyone knows everyone and they are enjoying each other's company. What a great place to be. But there in the middle, in full gaze of everyone is you—butt naked and alone. Not knowing anyone and with nothing to contribute. You don't even speak their language. And you are there for ever.

Is that where you want to be? No way. And God is not going to inflict it on you.

Today's Choices Matter For Ever

Jesus spoke about the need to choose between two roads. One of which leads to eternal life and the other to destruction.[62] These are his words, not mine.

He could well have been standing at such a junction when he said it. From the fork in the road two paths stretched into the distance and out of sight. Both had different destinations.

And there is no sitting on the fence. When you come to a place where the road divides you have to make a choice. Our greatest choice in life is to accept the road to forgiveness—so we can stand before him without shame.

I remember being given tickets to watch my team play in an important game. Unfortunately the seats were right in the middle of the other team's highly vocal fans. I have never felt so uncomfortable or so vulnerable. When our side scored it was bad enough—having to contain my joy. But when the other side scored it was even worse—having to pretend I was pleased.

It reminds me that in terms of our relationship with God there is no such thing as neutrality. We either trust him or we don't. We are either forgiven or we aren't. We either know him and are seeking to live his way, or we're not.

Can We Count on Jesus to Safely Deliver Us?

Jesus said of himself that those who believe in him would have eternal life.[63]

Like an adventurer on a journey to a foreign land—without the help of the latest and greatest SatNav system—you have to trust the guide.

He comes from the far and distant world and is intimately familiar with its uncharted and mysterious terrain. He has securely carried all those who have traveled before you to a safe arrival.

Go it alone and you'll be lost for ever. Trust the guide and he will deliver you with sure and certain security.

That's how I feel about Jesus. He has brought me forgiveness. And when the time comes to venture through the doorway of death, I trust him to bring me home—for ever.

12 BELIEVE IT OR NOT

Faith, foolishness or futility?

The words "faith" and "belief" haven't reared their heads excessively in the previous chapters. But you will certainly have smelt them between the lines.

After all, if what we have been exploring is going to be more than filed under "useful information" you are going to need to actually do something. And because that "something" doesn't involve anything you can actually see, touch, taste, hear or smell, it is going to involve "faith."

However, faith is a confusing business. We're told it can move mountains. But most people opt for dynamite and bulldozers. The cry goes up "keep the faith"—but what kind of container do they have in mind?

And there's all the stuff about blind faith and a leap of faith. Both of which can sometimes be responsible for some very strange behavior.

Take, for example, the motorist who tried to explain his car crash to a Munich court by saying he took his hands off the wheel because "I wanted to know, so I let go and asked: 'God, can you drive?'"

That bozo was only marginally dumber than the man who set the cruise control on his huge motor home—and went into the back to make a coffee. Which is also a true story.

What Faith Isn't

First things first, let's be clear about what faith isn't. Or, at least, let's be absolutely crystal so far as the kind of faith we are talking about here.

100

Faith is not in your genes

I've lost count of the times someone has said to me, "If only I had your faith"—as though I got more then my fair share at birth. Or that they didn't.

But faith is not a talent, dolloped out generously to some who then become "religious"—while others are for ever destined to be doubters. It's not something you inherit—like being able to sing in tune, wriggle your ears or learn a foreign language with ease.

The ability to exercise faith is like breathing, in that it comes as part of what it means to be human. After all, a loving God would never ask us to do something that is beyond our ability to achieve. To insist we believe when having no capacity to do so would be like throwing a stick for a legless dog and shouting "fetch."

Faith is not foolishness

Nor is genuine faith blind or irrational—abandoning ourselves to something that makes no sense at all. It isn't as one little boy sweetly said, "Believing in something you know isn't true."

The faith we are talking about is not like a placebo—that does you good even though there is no substance to it. Or just a nice fantasy that makes you feel better—like the idea that if I ever had a one-to-one with Gwyneth Paltrow she'd think I was rather wonderful.

Nor is real faith something that lacks a realistic foundation—as when an image of the face of Christ "miraculously appeared" on a wall in a Central American city and soon became a shrine with flowers and candles. The image turned out to be a poster for a Willie Nelson concert that someone had whitewashed over.

Three Kinds of Faith

Having nailed what "faith" isn't, there is still a bit of a maze to unravel. That's because the word is used in so many different ways it's easy to get confused. Let me try to untangle the knots.

Unconscious faith

There is a run-of-the-mill kind of faith we use 100 times a day without thinking. It happens automatically—in the same way that blinking is something we do without ever thinking about it.

We have faith that the letter we mailed will get there; faith that the seat will take our weight; faith that the date on today's newspaper is the right one. And when did you last insist on looking inside a box of cereal before you left the store just to make sure what was inside matched the picture on the front?

Of course, we may be let down from time to time, but this "automatic" faith basically keeps us going.

Sustaining faith

There is also a dimension to faith which involves us trusting in someone or something to come up with the goods on a regular basis. It may be faith in a rabbit's foot and the stars, or that everything works out in the end, or that good always wins, or in a God who cares.

This kind of faith is the expression of an attitude we have and it impacts the way we see life and respond to it. This is a moment-by-moment "sustaining" faith which impacts our actions and attitudes day by day.

Rescuing faith

This is an altogether different kind of faith; it's an act of faith that transforms our situation. It's the moment when you leap into the arms of the firefighter as the building burns. It's the decision to put yourself unreservedly into the hands of the surgeon. It's the commitment to trust yourself to the guide when you are lost and a long way from home.

And this is the type of once-and-for-all faith Jesus spoke of when he said, "Whoever believes in the Son has eternal life, but whoever rejects the Son will not see life, for God's wrath remains on him."[64] Jesus asks us to take what we believe about him and to express it as faith in him— which is rescuing faith.

Let's put it this way. You have just fallen into a large vat of slow-acting acid which will gradually eat into your body and destroy you. I don't know how it happened. Didn't your mother warn you about getting into a mess like this?

But here you are and your destruction is certain—unless you make a choice. And here comes the opportunity. To your door comes the Acid Antidote man—he also sells brushes and stuffed animals.

"I've got the very thing you need," he promises. "Stand on one leg and take a good swig of this."

"I don't like the color," you reply. "And maybe it won't work. And I'd feel such an idiot."

"It really will work," he insists. "It's been working for 2,000 years. And it's worked for me."

"Let me think about it," are your last words—and they may well be.

The help you needed was at hand but you refused to believe. The "wrath" of the acid is still active. You are in big trouble. Your future could have been very different had you acted with rescuing faith.

It Is What Our Faith Is In That Matters

The biggest issue of all is not the size of our faith. The biggest issue is who or what our faith is in.

For example, there you are about to leap from an airplane to make a sponsored parachute jump. You did the training, understand the techniques, and believe the physics of billowing parachutes will not let you down—other than gently.

For your first jump you were free to choose your own parachute—from three options. One had bloodstains on the outside and a tag saying "secondhand—one unlucky owner." The next had a note saying "Packed by the Scouts to raise funds." The third was in the hands of your instructor—he packed it himself and had double-checked everything.

Which one are you wearing? I thought so. Because it is what our faith is in that matters. In fact, that's all that matters. A small faith in the right parachute is never worth trading for an overwhelming faith in the wrong one. Take my word for it. Please.

When it comes to having our sinfulness forgiven and receiving the gift of everlasting life, Jesus is where our faith—however small—has to be placed. The same amount of faith in anything or anyone else will leave us unforgiven by God and without the eternal life he promised.

Faith Involves Action

Some years ago the Hoover Electrical Appliance company foolishly offered two free international flights to anyone living in the UK who spent at least £100 on an appliance. Unbelievable? But it was true—and I believed it.

Most of the people I knew believed too. But their belief didn't extend to action.

However, Hoover had said it. My wife, Rosemary, and I believed it. Oh, how we believed it. And we ended up with two free flights to Florida—all for the price of a vacuum cleaner we needed anyway. Meanwhile we lost count of the number of friends who said, "Well, you would!" But they could have—had they believed. I mean really believed.

It's like someone whose hands and face are caked with dirt and grime saying with a confident smile, "I believe in soap." Ask what they mean and they say, "Well, I believe soap is a good thing and to be much admired. I believe soap has made a great difference in world history. I believe soap has a lot to offer. I believe soap would get me clean if I were to use it."

In the same way, so far as Jesus is concerned, he does not ask us merely to admire the excellence of his life or the quality of his words. Rather he asks us to put his death on the cross to work in our lives—by faith.

Simple Steps to Faith That Rescues

There's a story Jesus told that helps to explain what faith that saves means. It centers on a son who left the family home after demanding—and receiving—the advance payment of his inheritance. He blew it all, and ended up having to eat pig food to survive.

Eventually the young man came to his senses and hit the road for home—planning to beg forgiveness and ask for a job as a servant in his father's home. Instead, the father—who had been watching and waiting—ran to embrace him, welcomed him back as his son and threw a humdinger of a party in his honor.[65]

Jesus told the story to explain the sheer joy in God's heart when those who have strayed from him come home. But it also conveys how rescuing faith works. Follow it through with me—because these are the steps each of us must take if we are to receive and experience God's forgiveness and to live as his children.

A realization of need. There, among the pigs and the swill, the young man faced up to reality. He was in a mess and totally unable to do anything about it through his own efforts. This is where our own journey toward rescuing faith has to begin. We need our eyes to be wide open to the reality of our own situation—which is that we are a long way from the Father's love and all that can bring.

A decision to seek forgiveness. Next, the son needed to make a decision. Something had to be done—and his only hope was to restore the relationship his selfish actions had destroyed. Our journey to forgiveness, like his, involves a decision to make a complete change of direction that will take us back to friendship with God our Father.

A turning from the mess of the past. The way forward wasn't a matter of improving the present by patching up things as far as was possible. It was about leaving the past behind in favor of a totally new start.

A dependence on the mercy of the Father. There was nothing the young man could do to change the situation through his own resources and power. His only hope was mercy from the one who had the ability to make the difference he needed.

An acceptance of the offer of forgiveness. When the father ran down the road to embrace him, the young man gladly received all that he needed. The past was forgiven, the relationship was restored, the future was certain.

A life as a son, not a servant. The ongoing relationship was not one of duty—like a servant to a master. But of kinship—like a father and a son.

Those simple but profound steps took a young man in desperate need into the loving and permanent embrace of his father's house. It's a picture of the journey we must take if the benefit of all that Jesus did on the cross is to be ours.

The Faith Transaction

If you are going to claim God's forgiveness and friendship for yourself through an act of rescuing faith, just how do you go about it?

Understanding our debt

Jesus wants to wipe away our guilt and to give us a new start. And his death on the cross was to make this possible. It was there he purchased an endless supply of forgiveness and now offers it as a completely free gift for us to receive.

Of course, that sounds unbelievable. Surely there must be something we have to do, some price we must pay, if we are to deserve such forgiveness. After all, everyone knows there's no such thing as a free lunch.

Can it really be that simple—with no strings attached? When you think about it, it has to be; no other answer is possible. Let me explain why.

Imagine you are the world's least successful kite-flyer—the Californian whose kite hit a high-voltage power cable, caught alight and fell to the ground. The fire it started destroyed or damaged 385 homes, engulfed 740 acres of brush, and caused 3,000 people to be evacuated. Total damage? Almost twenty million dollars.

Now what can you do? Will it be okay to say, "Sorry, let me write you a check?" Or, "Whoops—just leave it to me?" Just how much difference do you imagine it will make if you offer to spend your weekends helping out with a paintbrush? Or living on bread and water to provide funds toward rebuilding?

Meeting that kind of overwhelming debt is totally, completely, and utterly beyond you. And then some. There's only one hope. Mercy.

In terms of our spiritual needs we are in the same mess. There is an invoice bearing our name with so many zeros it defies comprehension. Attempting to settle it from our own resources—in either cash or kind—is like trying to bail out the *Titanic* with a thimble.

Identifying our rescuer

Our only hope is mercy—which is what Jesus provides through his death on the cross. There he established the currency of forgiveness—for us to draw down and apply, by faith, to our massively overdrawn account. But this forgiveness will never be credited to our account—and so pay our debt—until we ask him to make the transfer. And this is exactly where rescuing faith comes in.

Let me illustrate. I get a letter from the bank telling me I'm broke. Very, very, very broke. You don't need to know the gory details. But I'm in way over my head. I can't pay and there's no way I'll ever be able to. And to help even further, the letter informs me there will be a daily charge until I get out of debt. You've got the picture—it's going from bad to busted.

The thing is, I've got this benevolent Aunt Mabel and she's loaded— a bottomless money pit. I don't know where she got it all from—but boy, has she got it. And I need it—or at least some of it. And a note in her last Christmas card did mention that if I ever needed help I was to let her know.

So I write asking for help, owning up to being unable to meet my debts. I throw myself on her mercy. And that is exactly what I receive. Aunt Mabel helps me—by arranging for a money transfer from her account to mine via a check in my hand. When I see it there is another shock. Because not only will the payment clear my account in full but also provide me with enough to guarantee me everlasting credit.

Now here is where rescuing faith comes in. It's not enough to rec- ognize my need and ask for help—I have to take her at her word and present the check for payment. In the same way, we need to take hold of the blank check of forgiveness that Jesus created for us on the cross. We present it to God saying, "Here's payment in full." And God says, "You are forgiven."

And not only is our debt wiped clear—but our spiritual account is for ever treated as though it is the one belonging to Jesus himself. The bank balance of his perfect purity and sinlessness is credited to our account—for ever.

Taking the step

So here's the question—and there's none more important. Have you taken that step of rescuing faith? Or could it be you are still spiritually bankrupt—with the debt collectors at the door? If so, this could be the moment for you to cash the check of God's forgiveness. And God is waiting to hear from you.

My communication with rich Aunt Mabel was very formal with lots of posh words. That's not what God is looking for as we come to him. Your prayer may end up as little more than a desperate inner plea of "help" to God. That's no problem—when you reach out to him he hears your words but it's your heart he's listening to.

As you think about this important step in your relationship with God it may even help for you to create a picture in your mind. Imagine gathering all the unwanted junk in your life into a huge black garbage bag—or six—and putting it in the hands of God in exchange for his forgiveness. Or imagine all you wish was not true about yourself as though it were a wreck of a car—crushed into a cube—and traded in for a top-of-the-range model.

If you want some words to help you to frame what's going through your mind, the following could be appropriate. They are roughly what I said when I trusted Jesus for forgiveness.

Dear God,

I have hurt you, damaged others, and spoiled your world. I would like a new start and am now turning away from all I know to be wrong and setting my feet on the path to follow you.

Thank you that Jesus died on the cross to rescue me. I now receive the gift of your forgiveness that his death made possible.

Please make me new and come and live your life in me for ever.

Thank you for hearing this prayer and for answering it.

Remember, such a prayer is not a magic incantation—like wedding vows which make the event null and void if you miss out a key sentence. Stumble and splutter all you want. Find a quiet corner and just ache in God's presence if you must. But you can be confident he has the resources to forgive you, cleanse you, and to fill your life with himself.

There May Be Barriers to Believing

The decision to seize hold of God's offer of forgiveness and a new life by faith is vastly more significant than making up your mind to switch your deodorant brand or to show up in church more often. It demands even more than changing your allegiance to a football team or deciding to become a vegetarian.

And weighing up a step that is this significant—letting God rule and reign in your life—can raise all sorts of fears and barriers. Let me just touch on a few that might be making it hard for you to say "yes" to God.

Having to admit I'm wrong

It's been said: to err is human, to admit it is unlikely! And seeming to lose face with those we know well can be a sickening thought. For some who have vehemently argued there is no God, owning up to having been wrong can seem hard to stomach.

But sometimes owning up to the truth is the only thing we can do and still maintain our integrity. And it's not simply about owning up that you've been driving north for an hour when you should have been heading south. This is a matter of life and death.

What's worse—to look foolish, or to pass up the opportunity to become the person God created you to be?

There's still so much I don't understand

You may be thinking, "I'll jump when I know more." But how much more will be enough? If I'd waited to gain a degree in computer engineering I'd never have splashed out on a PC and transformed the way my life operates.

I still have many unanswered questions in the IT department. But I know what I need to know—and have the daily experience of learning even more.

In some ways the step of rescuing faith is a lot like marriage. At some point my knowledge about Rosemary was enough for me to make an initial commitment to marry her. By saying, "I will," I gave all I knew of myself—at the time—to all I knew of her—at the time. Looking back, I now see I didn't know much about either of us.

At that point I began a progressive commitment to her—getting to know her better as my wife and discovering how much she did, in fact, love me. My understanding has grown as I've trusted in her love and our relationship has developed. But if I'd waited until I knew everything it would have been a never-ending engagement.

What I've seen puts me off

It's just possible you've seen or heard about someone who seemed to become somewhat weird when they became a follower of Jesus. And you'd feel really uncomfortable having to speak and believe like them. To do so just wouldn't be "you."

The good news is that God doesn't expect you to be anyone other than who you are. Your comfort zones are fine by him. You don't have to behave like anyone else or feel what anyone else may feel. God respects each of us for who we are—as originals, not clones.

Jesus is the only door—but it's up to you whether you come in turning cartwheels or with a dignified stride.

What will others think?

The need to hang on to our credibility in the eyes of others looms large in all our thinking. To lay ourselves open to snide remarks about having become a Jesus Freak, or belonging in the loony bin, or retreating to the Dark Ages is no sane person's idea of fun.

Isn't it interesting that, in this present tolerant and anything-goes age, it is only following Jesus that evokes such comment? You can get more respect for believing in aliens, the power of crystals or claiming you're the reincarnation of Napoleon's horse trainer.

So you may well face the scorn and ridicule of others. It happened to those who first followed Jesus—and it has continued ever since. And it may not stop at name calling. Many have suffered deeply for their belief in Jesus—losing their reputation, livelihood, home, family, friends, and even life itself.

They made their choice based on the belief that there is nothing too great to sacrifice in order to know the forgiveness and new life that Jesus offers.

Take your pick—respectability and popularity, or the supreme joy of forgiveness and knowing God personally through Jesus. Of course, you can have both. But don't count on it.

I'll never live up to it all

It seems such a huge step to launch out on a new relationship with Jesus and with a determination to live the kind of life he designed you for—engulfed by honesty, integrity, faithfulness, and such. What if you severely mess up? Suppose the commitment you are thinking of making to put him first goes wobbly?

The truth is you *will* mess up and may well graze your spiritual knees as you take your first tottering steps in following Jesus. That's how it is for all of us who put our hand in his. And the reason is simple—those who follow Jesus are not perfect but forgiven.

And God is geared up to see you through. He's there—on your side—to help you make it and to forgive you when you don't. God's a loving father, not a prison warden. He also gives you the help you are going to need—as we'll see before this book is through.

The Heart of It All

There is nothing more central to this book than the issue of rescuing faith. So before we move on I want to make it as clear as I possibly can. So imagine you eventually arrive at the gates of heaven. You rub your eyes and admire your new white outfit—and move toward the gates to wait your turn.

Ahead of you each person is being asked the same question, "Why should God let you into his heaven?"

Up ahead you hear someone saying, "Well, why not? I've tried my best, been nice to lots of people, and never done anything really bad."

Another responds, "I've always helped others, and am pretty decent compared to most people."

And yet another says, "I've turned up at your place regularly and read your book and prayed a bit."

Yet, as you watch, each one has been turned away. Because there's a problem with answers like these—however sincere they may be. And it's a big problem. The keys that open the door of heaven are not those of "trying hard," "being sincere," "doing our best," and even "being religious." After all, if they were, there would have been no need for Jesus to die on the cross for us.

Or, to put it another way, if gaining a place in heaven can be achieved through our own efforts, then the death of Jesus can only have been one huge mistake.

Please be sure this has sunk in—because it represents the heart of all this book is about. Heaven is not a place where people walk around with pride because they earned the right to be there. It's filled with those who don't deserve it, but Jesus paid the price to let them in.

And now it's your turn. Take yourself back to that imaginary scene outside the gates of heaven. "Why should God let you in?" comes the question again. The only answer that brings a smile is, "Because I have placed my faith—my rescuing faith—in Jesus and the sacrifice he made for me on the cross."

I hope and pray that's the answer you would have in mind.

13 GRATEFUL DEAD

What could you be getting yourself into?

Did you jump? Pray the prayer? Place your faith in Jesus? For the moment I'm assuming you didn't and you are still running in "what am I getting myself into?" mode. And that's fine.

Yes, I do believe with every nid of my noddle that the decision in question is by far the most significant you will ever take. It's a life-changing, destiny re-routing resolution with no equal. And I'm not suggesting you should procrastinate about it.

However, spending small change takes hardly a thought. But when shelling out big-time—for a car, a new audio gizmo, a vacation, or whatever—I take my time over all the pros and cons. The bigger the decision, the more important it is to understand the consequences. And there's nothing bigger than this.

By the way, Jesus agrees with me—or perhaps that should be the other way round. When talking with those weighing up the prospects of following him, Jesus launched into a spiel about builders and armies. In effect he was telling them: When it comes to making up your mind, be like a builder who counts his bricks before he starts sploshing the cement; and be like a ruler who counts his soldiers before picking a fight.[66]

The message is, make sure you have what it takes. Don't end up a laughing stock—with the first few feet of your unfinished building permanently sticking out of the ground as an everlasting monument to your foolhardiness. Or like a ruler who has to live with everyone knowing he got pulverized for taking too few troops to war.

In both cases, of course, the builder and the ruler could have got it right—with a good dose of realism. And this is exactly where we are heading now. I'd like to help you weigh up all that's involved in following Jesus before you actually nail down your decision.

Naturally, if you have made the great step of placing your faith in Jesus—which is brilliant—you are still allowed to read on. Because there is some equally good news for you too.

A Covenant Commitment

Do you know what a "covenant" is? If I can make that clear then what follows will make so much more sense.

A covenant is a deal in which two parties say to one another, "I will if you will." Indeed, they do more than "say it," they pledge it. Each side promises to do their part, on the understanding that the other side will do the same.

Some contracts come close to the concept. Take that of a professional football player who pledges to train, play, keep out of trouble, and not mouth off to the media, while the club pledges to pay a stupid sum of money, watch over his family, keep the media off his back, and stand by him if trouble comes.

The act of marriage provides an even better example of a covenant in action. In response to the bride's vows you've never heard the groom reply, "That sounds like a good deal to me. I'll take it now. Let's go and eat."

Instead, both publicly lay out the terms of their mutual commitment to one another. They each say to the other, "I will," with every intention of doing just that. Each trusts the other will keep their vow. And this is what a covenant is all about. It's a two-sided mutually binding agreement between two willing parties.

What I'm leading you to is the fact that, throughout history, God has made a series of such covenants with his people on Earth.

One covenant was made with Moses when God gave the Ten Commandments. "I will be your God," said God, "if you honor me through these commandments." "We will honor you through these commandments," said the people, "if you will be our God."

Interestingly, the word for "covenant" in the ancient Jewish language—Hebrew—means to cut, or to shed blood. That's where the term "blood brothers" comes from. Two friends prick a finger, smudge the blood and *voila*! "I'm there for you and you're there for me through thick and through thin."

Blood brothers are made through "cutting a covenant." In the same way God "cut" a covenant with Israel when he gave the Commandments, except it was done through the blood of animals.

Jesus said that he came to introduce a new covenant[67]—one which was signed in his blood. Through his death, a new relationship with God became possible. Not on the basis of keeping laws and sacrificing animals—but based on the offer of free forgiveness through the death of Jesus.

Two-sided? God makes a commitment to us? Absolutely. And we'll come to all that this means in due time. But first, what is he looking for from us? If we are to turn from our self-centered, maybe very respectable but most certainly "me"-orientated life to follow Jesus, what is our side of the bargain?

I hope you are ready for a shock . . .

The Job Description Is "Disciple"

Let me take you to Jesus' recruitment office. There's a sign on the door saying "Disciples Wanted."

The word "disciple" is a close equivalent to what we call an "apprentice." The vacant position doesn't carry a mega-salary with all the perks. Instead, the working conditions promise an early start, long days, a minimum wage for a menial task and a prove-your-worth-by-keeping-on commitment.

Jesus was not out to gather the largest possible fan club. Instead of admirers he was after disciples. To him, the argument "Ten thousand people can't be wrong" meant nothing. Small could be beautiful if it was a genuine group dedicated to all he stood for.

Jesus knew people had a whole bunch of self-motivated reasons for following him. Some would just crave the excitement. Others, the buzz of something new. Others would see it as a way to power and significance for themselves. And, for some, the thought of free food for ever—even if it was only bread and fish—was motive enough.

He is not after volunteers, do-gooders, and those who think "Aren't you fortunate to have me among your number!" He is after those who, like an apprentice, will spend most of their time learning. They don't yet know much—but they know a man who does, and are following him.

But what about all this stuff about counting bricks and soldiers? What is it that being a disciple of Jesus lets us in for that may be beyond our resources?

As you saunter through the door of this mythical recruitment office you are confronted with posters that cover the walls. Each is emblazoned with one of the "come follow me" slogans Jesus used when speaking to the crowds that came to hear him. You're about to get the picture.

A Disciple Is Ready to Give Up His Own Life

The first to catch your eye is subtle in the extreme. "Anyone who does not carry his cross and follow me cannot be my disciple."[68]

Those who heard Jesus say these words knew exactly what he had in mind. It was a common sight to see those branded as criminals making their journey toward death with the equipment for their execution on their back. One day, Jesus would do the same.

There was no mistaking his message.

A disciple is one who is obedient. Look left again and there's another poster on the wall. "If you love me, you will do as I command."[69]

That's plain enough. Love and obedience, Jesus wants us to know, go hand in hand. The two are inseparable.

The word "obedience" probably evokes an image of dog training and obedience classes—and Jesus demanding we stop at the curb and respond to the command "leap." I can't help that—but it's a far from accurate picture.

What it means is that a disciple of Jesus salutes Jesus' flag, marches to his commands and checks out his orders of the day—and then does them.

An essential ingredient in a covenant is that both parties work for their mutual benefit. Sportsperson and club, husband and wife, are to act only in the best interests of the other.

"Jump," I yelled. And Rosemary jumped. Just in time to avoid the falling branch. She knew me well enough to know I wasn't playing games and that she wouldn't land in a pile of dog deposit. Though, to be honest, there was a time I told her to lick "ice cream" off a spoon when it was actually horseradish. But that was just for fun.

Being a disciple is not a matter of listening to the words of Jesus or even applauding them. Disciples listen and act. What could that involve?

Jesus spoke about forgiving those who wrong us, turning the other cheek, praying for those who are unkind to us; not fretting about how things will work out, and avoiding public display when we help others. He spoke of our need to be meek, merciful, pure in heart, and people who seek after peace. And a lot more besides.

He added that someone who failed to put his words into practice was like an incompetent buffoon who built his house on sand. So when the storms of life came—whammo. While the wise builder—the disciple—put them into practice, giving their life a solid foundation.[70]

Discipleship is a public issue. Don't think about following me unless you're ready to own me publicly, Jesus was saying. And remember, there may be more shame than gain.

In most societies of the world, it is simply not cool to be a disciple. You can get away with being nice in his name, joining the Christian club or dipping your toe in the water a little. But become a genuine disciple and your street-cred rating could plunge to zilch.

Suddenly you are at odds with the values and attitudes of a selfish me-centered society. You stick out like a very sore thumb. Not that you go looking for it. You don't have to. You just find most people are swimming in the opposite direction. They are dressed for leisure and you have your fatigues on.

And Jesus says, unless you are ready for that you are not ready to follow him.

Discipleship is a life and death issue. Those who carried their cross counted themselves as already dead. They had no plans for anything else. In the same way, Jesus calls us to die to our own selfishness, vain ambitions, and personal priorities.

The approach Jesus takes is in stark contrast to the advertising once used to recruit soldiers for the British army. Integrity would have meant a headline offering "Come and die for Queen and country." Instead a more palatable message appeared with an almost holiday-leaflet feel. The invitation? "Join the army and see the world."

Jesus is far more honest. But not too honest for our own good. He wants us to know exactly what we are getting into. With no false expectancy, no illusions, and no bargains.

Don't follow Jesus to find fulfillment—though I guarantee you'll find it. Don't follow Jesus for excitement—yet it will never be in short supply. Instead follow Jesus to "die." And sometimes this can be true in real terms.

Following Jesus means counting ourselves as dead to all that feeds our self-centeredness. Because he matters more than life itself. In fact, he is life itself.

A Disciple Is Ready to Say Goodbye to Everything

Eyes to the left and another poster hits you: "Any of you who does not give up everything cannot be my disciple."[71] Eyes to the right and there's another. "If anyone comes to me and does not hate his father and mother, his wife and children, his brothers and sisters—yes, even his own life—he cannot be my disciple."[72]

But surely Jesus doesn't want you to sell everything down to your underwear and, for good measure, to launch a hate campaign on those you love the most? You're right, he doesn't.

Jesus is using a style of Jewish speech that exaggerates something to the point of unreality to drive home a point. He did much the same with stories about people who had planks in their eyes and camels going through the eyehole of a needle.

But the points he makes are still big ones. He wants would-be disciples to understand two more vital things.

He's more important than anything we own. There is nothing worth clinging on to if it keeps us from following him. That's the message.

Disciples are asked to have the same attitude to life as their master. Jesus owned heaven and all its splendor. But, for our sake, he chose to die to all it offered. Instead of clinging on to his rights as God, he willingly became a man, humbling himself to die on a cross.

Jesus, who was rich beyond all our understanding, became poor so that we who are bankrupt could have his riches. All he had left in his hands were the nails that provide our forgiveness.

When what we own conflicts with following him, there is only one choice on offer.

He's more important than anyone we know. We are to love him so much it would almost seem to others that they were hated.

Let me allow Joseph to describe what this meant for him. He puts it this way

> In the Jewish home where I grew up, my family and I were very close. My relationships were so fulfilling—especially with my parents. We loved each other so, so much.
>
> Then, at the time when a young man and a father are growing closer—I became a believer in Jesus. I didn't realize just how this would impact the life of our family—especially the relationship with my father. When I finally got the nerve to tell them about my decision it didn't go down too well—it seemed my new-found faith especially hurt him.
>
> Of course, I wasn't trying to cause anyone pain. It's just that I couldn't deny I'd met a real, living person, whom I knew to be the Messiah I'd always longed for. I suppose my love for Jesus could have been mistaken for an act of rebellion toward my parents or a hatred of my Jewish upbringing. But it wasn't.
>
> It was just that I now had a very real relationship with the living God—something I could not, with all integrity, deny. I'm sure I could have handled it all more sensitively. But what had once been a close, sharing relationship with my father, became one of a strained silence for a number of years—causing great sadness for both of us.

Joseph had a choice to make. A costly one. And Jesus warns us that following him may demand the same for us.

Following Jesus is not about participating in his causes, cleaning up our act somewhat or showing our face more often on a Sunday. It's about putting our whole life under his control and making him the ultimate ruler of all we are, say, and do.

How this may work out will be very different for each of us. But the principle remains constant. To be a disciple means only the best will do. In God's terms, our very best is ourselves—all we are and all we have—made totally available to him.

Having looked so fully at what our side of the agreement involves, it's almost time to see all that God has for us as his part of the covenant. I can't wait to tell you. But first, one very important thing.

Behaving Like a Disciple Doesn't Get You to Heaven

It's important you don't misread me. You get no heavenly Brownie points by doing all the things a disciple is supposed to do.

Yes, the world will be a marginally better place if you act like a disciple. But no, it won't make you any more qualified for heaven than you are already. Being a disciple is not part of the journey toward the cross—it's the road that leads on from there.

If you try to behave like a disciple of Jesus in order to earn God's forgiveness you are in for a sore disappointment. The only person you're fooling is you—and your ego. And heaven isn't going to be filled with lots of self-righteous people feeling smug about earning the right to be there.

You can grit your teeth and obey everything Jesus taught, do everything he tells us to do and abandon everything you possess. But doing all these things will not give you the deep inner joy that comes from being a true follower of Jesus.

Sure, being a disciple is sometimes difficult and demanding. But the discipleship-journey is also marked by a wondrous covenant relationship with God—who gives abundantly more than we will ever need to follow him. Just how much more is what we are about to discover next.

14 MATHEMATICAL CERTAINTY

Does the other side of the equation add up?

The tune is—never going to make it onto my iPod—but the sentiment is right on the knuckle. Here we go, take a deep breath and join in. One, two, three . . . "All of me. Why not take all of me?"

Who do I have in mind to be singing it? You, perhaps? After all we've just been looking at together you'd probably think so. But no. It's not you but God himself I picture as the vocalist. And, for him, the invitation to "take all of him" is not some banal song lyric. He means every single word.

This is his part of the pact. His side of the covenant. As our blood brother he says, "Not only do I expect all of you. But you get all of me." What a deal. And how we need "all of" him.

No Hope For Loners

Think back to all that's expected of us as disciples. Does it all sound hard? How about "impossible"? You're right. Absolutely. It is quite outside our human ability to be the kind of faithful follower of Jesus he asks us to be.

Left with only the gas in our own tank and the grit in our own guts, we simply don't have the resources to love God and our neighbor with everything we've got. And nor do we have the inner strength to be the kind of person God desires, and to fulfill the plans he has for us.

So that's it then, is it? We've put our head above the parapet and decided it's not nice out there. Let's pack up the tent and go home. No, not a bit of it. Because God has the answer to our need—and that answer is himself.

121

He is Our Resource For the Journey

This is why God wants us to take all of him. Because it is all of him we need. Jesus calls us to follow him. We say "yes." God says, "You'll never make it without the right equipment. And I'm the equipment you'll need."

Have you ever watched a TV program on ocean racing or some epic journey to the frozen north? If so, you'll have seen the vast quantity of provisions stored on the boat or on the sleds. Every conceivable cranny gets stuffed with nourishing things. The provisions are built in at the very start of the design process, because they are essential to the team's success.

Our journey as followers of Jesus will be every bit as hazardous and demanding but God offers us all the equipment we need for our journey—himself.

To put it simply, when we commit ourselves to being followers of Jesus, God does not say, "Nice one. Make sure you keep it up." Instead he greets us with, "I'm going to come and live deep inside you and change you from the inside out."

In other words, when we become disciples we aren't suddenly handed a set of rules we must obey in order to remain a part of "the club." No, as disciples, we now have God living in us, giving us both the desire and the ability to live the kind of life we have always wanted, but have always been unable to experience.

Writing to those who were followers of Jesus, one of the very first Christian leaders put it like this, "the Spirit of him who raised Jesus from the dead is living in you . . ."[73] The same writer explained that God had "put his Spirit in our hearts . . ."[74]

Who and what is he talking about? About the Creator God—living in us. Why? Because we need God's power within us if we are to live a life that pleases him and brings us true happiness. As the same early Christian leader put it, "God will strengthen us with power in our inner being."[75]

So don't think for a moment that as you follow in Jesus' way, God is cheering from the sidelines like an adoring fan. Enthusiastically waving the fat foam "You're Number 1!" finger, caring enough to create a banner that says "Go, Go, Go!" but powerless to actually get the job done. God is not a cheerleader—God is actually running in our shoes.

I remember watching my son Joel zoom round a racing track at the wheel of a high-powered sports car. The experience was an eighteenth birthday gift. I was impressed—until his instructor changed places with him and took control. Then we saw what could be done and the motoring really began. But it was only possible because the one who could make the difference was in the driving seat.

And that's where we need God to be at work. Within us. At the very heart of all we are. And for three good reasons.

They're Out to Get Us

Think of it like this. You're a hollow tin ball being used for the squash championship of life. I know squash balls aren't made of tin, but humor me. And there are three finalists putting you through the school of hard knocks.

Finalist number one—the world. He's a fall-in-with-the-crowd—a real people pleaser and wants to entice you to be one too. Subtlety is his strength—full of flicks and drop shots. No wonder he's world champion.

Most people dance to his tune and he wants to trap you into doing the same. To have the same values and attitudes. What do I mean?

This guy lives as though *this* life is all there is—that there is nothing beyond what we experience with our five senses. He believes what we own is the only way to measure what we're worth—just like the great crowd of his God-ignoring fans.

He mutters as he whacks you with his racket, "Forget God and do what everyone else is doing—just keep on bouncing, bouncing, bouncing . . ."

Finalist number two—the flesh. The name doesn't sound very nice—and he isn't. He's a pig of a player. Plays dirty, breaks the rules, and has to—because he's not much good at what he does. He's constantly out of control—and leaves a trail of mess and destruction behind wherever he goes.

He's your own inner nature—which infects all you do with a tendency toward pride and a belief you can do it all yourself. He'll trip you up time and time again.

What makes him one of the more devastating players is that he has the ability to blame his faults on others. The opponent, the referee, the crowd, his potty training. He may look good—but he is rotten to the core. He will rot you from the inside out and take you down.

Finalist number three—the devil. Forget pictures of pitchfork, horns, and spiky tail—this guy looks great. Mister "lean and agile"—with the smug smile of a used car salesman. Don't underestimate his power to hit you out of the court—he's fast, fit, and furious.

He has no end of schemes up his T-shirt to keep you bouncing around—dented and distracted from thinking about God for ever. His smash is devastating. And he just keeps on coming at you—especially when you are not expecting it.

These three enemies are what make following Jesus impossible under your own steam. And as they put your life as a tin squash ball through its paces you'll get a real beating. Long before your four-score years are up you will look more like a cheese grater than a squash ball. Dented, dinged, damaged, and drilled through with holes from bends, breaks, and bad bounces.

That's why we need God to come in with his strength and power. How different the game would be if your tin shell was fortified with a solid new core—that filled you and pushed out all the dents and dings.

And that's what God wants to do—pour his presence into you like molten steel. And so transform you into something entirely new— restored to a perfection better than when you were first created, and with a perfect bounce.

That whole tin squash ball routine is a daft picture. But it expresses the astounding truth that, as we follow Jesus as his disciples, God comes to live in us. His solid presence within transforms us into an entirely different person—inside and out.

Back to the Factory

But why are we born as hollow tin balls in the first place—instead of burly ball bearings? Wouldn't that have been better?

Jesus explained why to a great religious leader named Nicodemus. The man was one of the more respected rule-keepers of Jesus' day and sincerely wanted to know God better and to live in a way that pleased him.

Jesus said some radical things to him. And he also says them to us. So imagine you're sitting there face to face with Jesus just like Nicodemus was—and needing the same answers.

You say, "Jesus, you know I try to play by all the rules. I'm pretty okay—and yet there is something missing at the very center of my life. Can you help me?"

Jesus says to you, "You've had that problem since you were born. And it's one you never noticed.

"You see," he continues, "when you were born you were physically alive and fine. But there was a major problem at your birth. Your spirit was stillborn. Though your body was alive, your spirit was unable to experience the love I have for you. In other words, your spiritual heart did not start beating and it hasn't started yet."

The only answer, Jesus explains, is to be born spiritually in the same way you were physically. Having been born from the womb you now need to be born from the Spirit.[76]

If you are to come alive to God you must allow him to place a new spirit within you—his Spirit. In doing so he creates for us all what was done for that imaginary tin squash ball—only more.

Imagine a shape like the English letter Y. If it had no center it would simply fall apart. Our lives are like that—falling apart without God filling our birth defect, the spiritual hole in our heart.

God's plan is to make us completely new people. He longs to give us a brand new heart—solid to the core, able to love and be loved, full of all we need for life in all its fullness—full of God himself.

God In Three Persons

To help you grasp the immensity of what it means to have all that God is on our side and within us, I need to unpack what it means for God to be a trinity. This is slightly technical stuff. But it's worth it—because there's even more to God than you have yet to discover.

You'll have heard the word "Trinity." Or phrases like "the Holy Trinity—Father, Son, and Holy Spirit." And probably been as confused as most people about what that could mean! It's not a word Jesus ever used and neither did his earliest followers. But gradually it became a useful way of identifying what they all knew to be true.

The issue is this. While there is but one God, he is three persons—God the Father, God the Son, and God the Holy Spirit. All are equal. All are the same. All have different roles and functions. They are inseparably separate. They are at one and are one—yet they are three.

Please forgive the simple picture, but understanding God as Trinity is kind of like the way we use three names for H_2O. When we want to drink it, we call it water. When we want it frozen so we can make another drink cold, we call it ice. And when we want it hot to get the wrinkles from our clothes, we call it steam. But it's always H_2O.

If H_2O makes understanding the Trinity as clear as mud—try it this way

- God is God—and Jesus spoke of him as Father.[77]
- Jesus is God—and God spoke of him as "my son."[78]
- The Holy Spirit is God—which is the way Jesus spoke of him.[79]

For centuries, the early disciples used a symbol shaped like our English letter Y to remind them of all that God is and to help them understand the concept of God as Trinity. Three prongs—but one letter. Three persons—but one God.

Those who knew Jesus and followed him came to be in no doubt that both Jesus and the Holy Spirit were God, as much as the Father was God. And they constantly spoke of the three in the same breath—just as Jesus had done.

So how come, if there are three persons who are God, we can still talk about there being only one God? Surely there must be three? After all, the math is easy: 1+1+1=3.

But try the sum this way: 1x1x1=? Right—One!

It is this three-person God who invests himself in us.

The Father—The Perfect Parent

Jesus told his followers to speak to God as "Our Father."[80] And Jesus himself used the word "*Abba*"—a Hebrew word meaning Daddy[81]—in conversation with his Father in heaven. And there was hardly a more intimate word in his vocabulary than the one toddlers first utter while hugged in their father's embrace.

Of course, in human terms fathers are a mixed bag. I'm not everything my kids hope for and deserve—nor was my own father. But God is the perfect parent. He is everything we wish our human parents had been and more.

He's always there for us, always has time, always does what is in our best interests. And as the one with inexhaustible supplies of everything—he has a bottomless well of love, patience, compassion, and fairness.

He loves us no matter what. The mark of a true parent is to love and keep on loving. No matter how wayward and rebellious any of my kids may turn out to be, I'd like to believe there's nothing they could ever do to stop me loving them.

This is even more true with God. His love is strong enough for him to sacrifice his son for us. And it's the foundation of our whole relationship with him.

He's at work on our behalf. Ask your heavenly Father for whatever you need, said Jesus, and you will get it.[82] Of course, there's a considerable gap between what we want and what we really need. And God's assessment of our need can be different again from ours.

As a loving Father, God listens and answers—with our very best interests always on his heart. But of course, it's those who know him as Father who are invited to pray "Our Father." There's a vast difference between my children asking me for something and their friends making the same request.

My kids get special treatment and so do we.

The Son—The Image of the Father

When Jesus left the Earth at the end of his resurrection appearances his work was not over.

He holds us in his grasp. "No one can snatch my sheep out of my hand," Jesus promised his disciples.[83] The hands that created the universe—the same hands that were nailed to the cross—now hold us firmly in their grasp. No matter how many times we fall or fail, Jesus loves us and remains committed to helping us follow him and experience his love.

It's like a child holding onto his father's hand while crossing a busy street. At least, that's what it looks like. But, in reality, that little hand is firmly encased in one that will never let it go. And that is how secure Jesus keeps his own. His love will never let us slip from his grasp.

The Holy Spirit—Our Helper

You may think it doesn't look as though Jesus is doing a whole lot now that his work on Earth is finished. Yes and no. He has a lot to do—but he's delegated!

Just before he was arrested, and the journey toward crucifixion began, Jesus made a promise to his disciples that he would send them a replacement for himself—one who would provide everything they needed to be his disciples.[84] He would send them the Holy Spirit.

Their job was to live God's way and to turn others to the same path. Yet Jesus, the one who was the very center of their lives, was leaving them. They needed something—or someone—special.

Jesus told them they would be drenched or submerged[85] in the Holy Spirit—like a sunken boat which has water inside and out. As the disciples said "yes" to God by giving themselves to him, God would say "yes" to them by filling them with his presence and power.

As he spoke to them, Jesus made it clear that the Holy Spirit would be everything those who followed him would need after he had gone.

The Holy Spirit is our constant helper. As Jesus' time on Earth was ending, he promised to send his Holy Spirit so every disciple would have him with them all of the time, wherever they were.[86]

Today, God lives in each true follower of Jesus through his Holy Spirit—including you, if you ask him to. He will be with you to help you all the time and in every situation—no matter how demanding or difficult. Seven days a week.

The Holy Spirit reminds us of what we hear. There's a supernatural dimension to learning and understanding the truth about God—and the Holy Spirit makes it happen. Through his help we remember more of what we have heard and learned about God than we would have thought possible.

It's remarkable. Time and again, when I need it, some aspect of what I've heard or learned about God suddenly pops into my brain from I know not where—except that I do know where. The Holy Spirit is at work.

And he will do exactly the same for you if you trust him too.

The Holy Spirit teaches us what we need to learn. The Holy Spirit opens our understanding to the truth about God. Which is how uneducated people like the first disciples made such an impact.

The limit to what God can teach you and do through you is not your memory, intelligence, or education. It is your willingness to allow the Holy Spirit to teach you.

I've lost count of the times I've heard people say "Now I get it" about a vital spiritual issue they had never understood. It always excites me to see God, by his Spirit, doing what he promised—opening our minds to what is true about him.

If a lot of what I'm talking about in this book makes as much sense as alphabet soup, don't panic. The Holy Spirit is ready to make it clear to you— as he has done through the ages to millions of others.

The Holy Spirit gives us the power we need. What were the followers of Jesus like after his execution? They were just a very ordinary group of people—frightened, disillusioned, with all their great hopes and dreams at an absolute end.

What was going to transform them into a dynamic group who would go on to turn the world upside down? It wasn't a management course on self-belief. It wasn't an extreme makeover. It wasn't willpower. No, it was the power of the living God within them.

That power is an inner strength to be and do what's simply not possible through our own abilities. It includes

- Having courage beyond our expectations in difficult situations
- Finding the strength to go on when humanly we've run out of road
- Developing a character like that of Jesus himself—through the qualities of love, patience, self-control, joy, serenity, and so on growing in our lives
- Receiving special abilities—a few or many—to use in the service of God, his people, and the world: from being better able to explain more clearly what we believe, to being great at administration or hospitality; from the ability to worship him with all we've got, to the strength to die for him if it comes to it.

On the fence at the end of my neighbors' garden—the nice neighbors who don't have an insomniac dog with a howl that causes birds to fall from the sky—is a "plastic man with a windmill thing." The man holds a crank handle that is joined to the windmill. And when the wind blows, the windmill turns and the man cranks.

Except that it looks to be the other way round. At first sight, it appears that the man is doing all the work. When the wind blows I could almost swear I see that little man grin, flex his arms, crack his knuckles, and begin to crank himself into a macho sweat. That's how it is when the Holy Spirit is at work in us. He does the work and we get to look good.

Without the Holy Spirit's presence, a disciple of Jesus would be like a sail without the wind. The Holy Spirit makes following Jesus possible.

The Holy Spirit helps us be sure we are God's child. Perhaps, above all else, you wonder how you could possibly ever know God has heard your prayer asking him to rescue you and come into the center of your life.

Maybe you have prayed such a prayer and you didn't hear the angels break out into the Hallelujah Stomp. Or maybe you did—and are confused.

Again, this is where the Holy Spirit goes to work. One of the most wonderful things he does is to help us know, deep within us, that we now belong to him.

Of course, that step of rescuing faith happens in different ways for different people. For some it is a very dramatic moment. They can tell you exactly when and where it took place and even the color of the wallpaper in the room at the time.

Others, like me, find they gradually reach a point where they can look back and realize they are trusting in Jesus and not themselves for their future with God.

Some are as cool as a cucumber. Others weep buckets. My daughter Xanna asked me, "Does it tickle a bit when you ask Jesus to come into your life?" because for her it had. Others just have a great sense of relief over having finally settled the matter.

I picture it like crossing the equator. Some mark the dramatic moment with great ceremony and a glass of bubbly. Others look back only to realize it has already happened. But both have passed from one side of the world to the other.

When it comes to being sure, whatever your experience—or lack of one—several things remain true.

- You will begin to see signs of change in your life—old attitudes will start to go and new desires begin to grow. In effect you'll begin acting like a butterfly instead of a caterpillar.
- What you hear about God will increasingly make sense—and you'll grow hungry for more.
- You will start to experience a deep inner peace.
- You'll see the world with clearer eyes and a fresh perspective. Life will take on a quality that you had never thought possible.

But far above anything that may or may not happen to you, remember one thing. God can be trusted to keep his promises. You may not feel different, but that does not change the fact that God has promised you his forgiveness if you ask for it and will keep his word.

Whether or not I feel married doesn't make an inch of difference to what's true. Two people said "yes" and that settled it. If you've said "yes" to God and meant it he has most definitely said "yes" to you.

A Final Chorus

You've looked at the challenge of what it means to be a disciple of Jesus. You've seen how God wonderfully makes himself available to provide all you need to live it out.

So could it be the time to burst into song? With God and you singing in perfect harmony. "All of me. Why not take all of me."

Or, make it a prayer along the lines of

God, here I am with all my doubts, confusion, and failures. I'm asking you to come and grasp me in your arms. Please take me as I am and make me what you want me to be. Clean me up from inside out and fill me up with everything you are.

Or you may want to flick back to the prayer in chapter 12, page 113 of this book to make your commitment. There is an adventure waiting.

15 THE GAME OF LIFE

Is it okay for rules to rule?

Having come this far you may be wondering "What next?" You've decided to give God your "yes" but now what? Could it be you see yourself needing to save up for a copy of that much to be treasured book, *Two Thousand Ways to Keep God Happy, Vol. 1*, bound nicely in black?

That's my assumption because many who set out to follow Jesus have an assumption of their own . . . that the road ahead is littered with rules and regulations. That it's going to be a bit like playing some great new board game where we open the box and—first things first—study the rules. Before we know where we are, we've stacked up loads of them. Things we must do, should do, dare not do, feel compelled to do—if we are to keep God happy.

If that's anything like the way you are seeing it, I have some great news. You couldn't be more wrong.

There Is Nothing We Can Do to Earn God's Love

A good friend of mine tells of being on a long flight to some far-flung destination. In the seat in front a girl of about four kept bouncing up and down singing, "I'm going to see Daddy. I'm going to see Daddy"— all the while filling her face with candy bars.

As the plane came in to land the child vomited spectacularly down her pretty "Daddy will love this" dress. And my friend could not wait to see what kind of reunion would result.

The outcome was as splendid as it was surprising. The two rushed toward each other over the terminal carpet. With the business-suited father, oblivious to the onrushing stench, enfolding the puke-covered child into his arms with the cry, "That's my girl."

What mattered wasn't how sweetly the child smelled—or how many rules she had kept. It was all about their relationship as father and child—and there was nothing that could change that.

It's a great picture of the kind of relationship we have with God when we come to follow Jesus. As one of the world's leading God-thinkers has put it, "God simply is nuts about you." There is nothing we can do to earn God's favor and cause him to love us more. His love is at full stretch already.

God's love comes to us without conditions. He does not say, "I love you if . . ." He just says, "I love you"—unnerving as it is in a world that believes there's no such thing as a free lunch. But with God, that's all that is on offer.

God's Love Goes On the Way It Started

The world over, people imagine the only way to relate to God is through the things they do. By being good enough often enough. Yet the first step to a living relationship with God is to grasp that only the goodness of Jesus can meet our needs.

And if that's the "first step" it is also the second step and the third and the . . . Because that's the way it stays after we put our faith in Jesus and have begun to follow him. In the same way that we couldn't earn points with God before we were forgiven, we can't earn them now. And God doesn't ask us to.

Is that reasonable? Absolutely not. God's love for us is the most unreasonable thing in the universe. It was his unreasonable love that sent Jesus to the cross for you. It is his unreasonable love that continues to burn for you, no matter what. God loved you unreasonably when you spent most of your time ignoring him. And he is just as unreasonable now that you have set your head, heart, and mind to follow him.

We have never deserved God's love and will never deserve it. But he just keeps on loving us anyway. Because that's the kind of God he is. It's in his DNA.

Rules Are Not God's Plan

That's why God hates man-made rules that just involve duty.

When Jesus was on Earth, the Pharisees—the religious lawmakers—had cornered the market in rule-making and policing law-breaking. They had hundreds of petty rules, like how much you could greet a bride on her wedding day, and how much you could console a widow at her husband's funeral. To keep all these rules was like trying to pat your head, rub your belly, do a somersault, flip a pancake, and tie your shoes—all at the same time. Except just a bit harder.

Catch this—there were even rules about what you could use to lower a bucket into a well on the day of rest, the "Sabbath." The verdict was you couldn't use rope, as this would constitute work. But the rules did allow you to tie your bra as that was necessary for modesty. So you could tie a bra to a bucket and get water from the well that way.

That's where you can get to when you use rules as the basis of a relationship with God. And it is all too easy to find ourselves heading in the same direction. Out of the sincerest of motives we try to earn God's love and forgiveness by religiously keeping a set of rules.

Jesus used the strongest language to denounce these kinds of shenanigans. The Pharisees caught the sharp edge of his tongue because of the way they tied the people up in knots—or bra straps—with the endless petty rules they gave out for pleasing God.

You can easily understand why.

Rule-keeping is based on pride. In keeping rules, Jesus said, the Pharisees were trusting in their own ability to earn God's love, rather than resting in the passionate love God had for them all the time. They wrongly believed they had something to contribute to the equation. It can be the same for us.

Rule-keeping rejects God's love. Imagine how you would feel if, time after time, the person you loved so deeply never accepted it. Instead, they continually behaved like an obsessive-compulsive idiot in order to try and make you love them—when you already did.

When Jesus calls out to us in love, it is not to a whole new set of rules, but to a whole new way of life—a life of rest from the struggle to earn love.

If Not Rules, What?

When Jesus set out his plan for those who follow him he made no mention of the compulsory wearing of open-toed sandals and singing "Kumbaya". Or how often to pray, how much to give to charity or how many fish symbols to put on your car. Instead he spoke of our goal as to "Love the Lord your God with all your heart, soul, mind, and strength, and love your neighbor as yourself."[87]

That's a pretty broad and exciting landscape to be traveling over. It involves putting the best interest of God and others at the top of our priorities—and doing so with energy and enthusiasm. And not because there are rules involved but because this is the most fun there can be this side of heaven.

A *living relationship*

Instead of rules, God has called us to a relationship with him. Let me explain it this way. The ushers have asked each guest, "Are you with the bride or the groom?" Now the happy couple begins to exchange vows before the assembled multitude and you can hardly believe your ears.

"Do you, Dwight, promise never to leave your toenail clippings on the bedroom floor, to always take out the trash, always rinse round the bath after you've used it, never to do the crossword when it's not your turn, always to put the toilet seat down when you've finished, to say please and thank you in a cheery voice—even when you have toothache, to . . ." The vows that follow from Petunia are equally detailed and rule-based.

Of course, you've never heard anything like it. That's because the basis for marriage is not rules but a relationship—with the significant commitments to honor, worship, obey, cherish, share, and so on.

In the same way, this is what God has in mind for us. He wants a relationship based on our mutual needs and expectations. A relationship where we get to know him better, understand his ways more clearly, and live accordingly. And none of that is about rules.

It is here that I'd like to tell you a true story—though I am not free to give you all the details because this would risk the safety of those involved.

During the horrendous Rwanda tribal massacre, Elizabeth (not her real name) saw her son brutally murdered by a soldier. Though

devastated, she agreed with a Christian working with a local develop-
ment agency that they should pray together for the killer to own up to
what he had done.

Not long afterwards, that is exactly what happened. Her son's killer
came to her, his gun in his hand, saying he could not get her image out
of his head. "Take me to the authorities," he asked her. "So I can be
punished as I deserve."

The grieving woman had another response. His "punishment" was to
take the place of her son and for her to lavish love and care on him.
And that is how they are now living.

I can think of no more graphic a way to convey what God has done
for us than that remarkable story. Because of us Jesus had to die.
And God's response is to take us into his family and lavish his love on
us.

I can just imagine how that forgiven soldier is behaving in his new
home—and it has nothing to do with rules. Instead, out of love and gratitude he simply wants to please the one he now serves as a son in
every way possible. And that's how it is for us.

Accepted as we are

So what about those things we feel we "ought" to do because they will
improve our relationship with God? Where do rules come in here?

Let me give you an example. Let's say you agree with God that at a
specific time each day, you'll spend some time alone focusing on him
in your thoughts and with the aid of the Bible. That's not a bad idea, but
there are two ways you can approach this commitment.

You can say, "I will spend time with God like this because he loves
me and I love him and it's great to talk." Or you can say, "I'm going
to do this to make sure he will keep on loving me and being nice
toward me, and because I know others who do it and feel I ought to
as well."

It's the motive behind keeping these "rules" that's important.

This means we don't have a duty to meet with others who follow
Jesus. It's our joy to do so—because it's great to be with those who are
as grateful for God's love as we are. And it's not our duty to pray—it's
just brilliant to be able to talk to the One who loves us so much. It's not
our duty to tell others the good news about Jesus—it's something that
just happens when we have had such love poured upon us.

What About When We Fail?

There will be many times when we don't live up to our goals and aspirations. After all, setting out to "Love the Lord your God with all your heart, soul, mind, and strength, and love your neighbor as yourself" can be kind of stretching. And there's nothing to feel guilty about when we fall short of what we are aiming at—unless others get hurt in the process.

It's okay to aim for the stars and hit the moon. Or to plan to read the whole Bible in a year and only get half way. This is not something to feel deeply guilty about.

However, there will be times when our failure is actually sin. Because, despite our growing desire to love God and others, there will be times when we don't. So what then?

The answer revolves round the two kinds of relationship that we have with God when we become a follower of Jesus. Two? Yes, two.

The two relationships I have with God are like the two relationships I have with any one of my five children. First there's the legal relationship—by birth. And there is nothing they or I can do to change it even if sometimes they may feel they want to.

In the same way, through faith in Jesus, we become adopted by God as his child. As John put it in his gospel, "to all who received him [Jesus], to those who believed in his name, he gave the right to become the children of God."[88]

That relationship is irreversible and unbreakable too—no matter what you may do.

The other father and child relationship I have is exactly that—a "parental relationship." It can be close and intimate. Or strained and even broken. But all the time our legal relationship remains intact.

What it means, for example, is if one of my offspring hurls a bowl of cornflakes across the breakfast table at me they would still be my child—but it wouldn't be a good moment to ask me for a new bike for Christmas.

That's how it can be with us, as God's children. From the moment we trust Jesus for forgiveness and begin a new relationship with God we become God's child. And that legal relationship can never change. However, there are times when our willful or thoughtless behavior impacts that relationship. It makes him sad and gives us a sense that we're no longer close to him.

What we need when that happens—and it will—is a way back. And God has made it possible.

Flossing or a Root Canal?

It is here that dental hygiene comes to mind. Mostly, my gnashers need no more than a daily floss. But, just occasionally, something more drastic is needed. It's a bit like that when it comes to keeping our spiritual breath smelling sweet in God's nostrils.

Let's start with the heavy stuff first; the root canal territory.

There could come a time when you mess up big-time in the loving God and neighbor stakes. And the temptation is to think, "That's it, there's no way back." It's then that you need to think about what happened to one of Jesus' best friends—the disciple, Peter. He made more of a mess of things than you could imagine.

Peter was convinced he'd never let Jesus down. So much so, when Jesus said all his friends would one day deny knowing him, Peter protested, "No way, Lord. I will die with you before I deny you."

Jesus had a more realistic view and said, "You will deny me Peter—even three times before the rooster crows in the morning."[89]

Within hours Jesus was arrested and Peter fled with all the others. Then, as he sneaked back to see what was going on with Jesus, Peter swore blind to three different people who recognized him that he was no way a follower of Jesus.

And then the rooster crowed.

Three strikes and Peter was out. Jesus turned and looked right into Peter's eyes. And Peter slunk away in shame, weeping bitterly.[90]

For Peter that could well have felt like the end of the story. And there can be times when we feel that too. But it wasn't and it needn't be for us.

Soon after Jesus rose from the dead, he and Peter again came face to face. Peter may have been dreading it, expecting to get both barrels. But all he received was love, forgiveness, and a new start.

It happened after Peter and his fellow disciples had been fishing all night. The risen Jesus began calling to them from the beach. Recognizing the voice, Peter plunged into the water and swam ashore. And over the breakfast of fish that he'd cooked, Jesus asked, "Peter, do you love me?" Not once but three times. Not in anger but in love. Not to condemn but to welcome him back.

Jesus was helping Peter move on from his failure. "Yes, Lord I love you—you know that I do,"[91] Peter replied, each time stronger than the last.

All Jesus was interested in was seeing Peter back on the road again. It's the same for us. Jesus did it for Peter and he always wants to do it for us. But how?

If we confess our sins

We know God never winks at sin. It's too much of a stench in his nostrils for that to happen. And its impact is too profound to be ignored. This is why the death of Jesus was so essential. It was a sacrifice for all sin for all time—even for my sins that are still to come.

The death of Jesus provides a limitless reserve of forgiveness for the future—against which we can cash each and every IOU that our continuing sinful behavior creates. Obviously this only applies to you if you have taken that step of "rescuing faith" in Jesus. It is only then you have an endless line of credit on your account waiting to be drawn down.

How does that work? Another one of Jesus' great friends, John, wrote, "if we confess our sins to God, he can always be trusted to forgive us and take our sins away."[92]

That's how it works with the root canal activity that's needed when we mess up big-time. But it is exactly the same in the flossing department. The kind of daily confession we need—to clear out those bits that would build up and hinder our day-to-day relationship with God.

Of course, "confessing our sins" means a lot more than mechanically running through a list. It is about "doing a Peter." Peter was truly sorry for what he had done and wanted to get it sorted. And the sorrow he felt was linked to the love he had for Jesus and the hurt he had caused him.

Confession for us comes out of that same kind of deep, personal sorrow for the damage done to our relationship with God. And a genuine longing not to repeat the past. It involves agreeing with God that what we did, said, or thought was wrong. And thanking him for forgiving us.

When we do genuinely confess our sins to God—as Peter did—he acts faithfully and justly. This is possible because the payment for our wrongdoing has been made. We are again made clean—as clean as Jesus.

Can We Do What We Like and Then Say Sorry?

Some people are daft enough to suggest that, because "sorry" is enough, we can get away with murder in God's eyes. But how could anyone who has received such love at so great a cost then willfully exploit it?

If someone risked life and limb to save me from some terrible fate, would I steal their wallet? If someone offered a blank check to pay off all my bills—at great personal expense—would I first go on a luxuriously indulgent spending spree?

In the same way, if I have really understood the passion of God toward me, how could I possibly keep hammering the nails into the hands and feet of Jesus knowingly and willingly? No way.

Some of the first followers of Jesus so misunderstood how much God loved to forgive that they decided to do him a favor—by giving him lots of opportunities to do so. They deliberately did wrong so God would have the pleasure of showering them with forgiveness.

However bizarre that may sound, at least they had grasped the big issue—that God delights in forgiving. Like the story Jesus told about the father who welcomed back his waster of a son, God will do the same for us, time and time again. But like that son, we would never exploit the love of the Father.

One Step Backwards—Two Steps Forward

Think for a moment of your new life with God as though it were a garden. Over the past few pages of this book we have discovered how sweet the flower of God's mercy smells. And how God helps us deal with the weeds that grow in our life.

But there's even more to it than that. God's plan is not just for you to exist, but to flourish and grow. How? Please follow me to the greenhouse.

16

IT'S A PLOT

How will your garden grow?

We begin our journey of faith by coming to know God—and continue the journey by getting to know him better. It's a bit like moving to a foreign destination in that arriving is only the start of it. Now comes the excitement of exploring.

But when it comes to "exploring God," how do we do it? Is it just down to reading the guidebooks and talking to the natives? Or is there more?

With that thought in mind, let me run a couple of questions by you—in the hope they will expand your horizons and expectations.

Question 1: If God intends us to have a relationship with him, how can we get to know him better? Question 2: If God is a person he must have plans, purposes, and intentions—for us and for others. So how can we get in on them?

Those are the questions. Now let's go digging and rummaging through the dirt for some answers.

Nurturing Our Relationship With God

As we are thinking of you as a "newish" follower of Jesus, it could be appropriate to use the imagery of the nursery to make things clear. But I find projectile vomiting, potty training, and grazed knees somewhat off-putting. So instead, let's transplant you into a garden as a fledgling plant.

Forgive me if I flog the horticultural image to death over the following pages. But there's so much we can understand about our relationship with God and his people through the insights of a garden.

141

We've already seen that our life with God is to be a relationship. So how do we make that work?

It's Good to Talk

Some while ago Prince Charles hit the headlines for allegedly talking to plants. It appears he'd bought into the theories of Dr. Gustav Theodor Fechner, a German professor, who believed people should have a regular heart to heart with their plants to help them grow.

True or not, there are those who do exactly that—defending themselves with the claim that plants have feelings too. These person-to-plant chit-chats are supposed to make both parties healthier.

To me that all sounds completely hibiscus. But whether or not a plant benefits from a friendly chat, our relationship with God most certainly does. Such conversation is like the oxygen that every healthy plant needs to grow.

Most people call this kind of conversation "prayer"—but "prayer" is a word that can conjure up strange notions. We may assume it involves learning a whole new vocabulary, going to special places, reciting things written long ago, doing something with our body we are not particularly used to, and even putting on a special voice that would get us some very funny looks if we were out in public.

None of that need be true. Think of it this way.

Prayer is not a ritual. There are those who can only ever enter the presence of royalty fully booted and suited and accompanied by a full monty of pomp and circumstance. Yet, down through the years, some have swooped unannounced into the presence of a royal personage wearing their Harrods jim-jams, and yelling "Daddy" or "Mummy" as the case may be.

In the same way, although you can't get any more majestic than God, he has also made himself known as our Father in heaven. And that's the basis of our time in his company. We don't engage in an audience with a head of state, but enjoy time with a loving father.

Of course, our visiting rights with God should be respectful. But we do go to him as his child and that's how he wants it.

Prayer is a conversation. When chatting with friends there are times when we are serious—even crying. At other times we are earnest. And often, we just enjoy each others' company. Our conversations with God can be much the same.

"But I will run out of things to talk about," you feel. And you might. In which case you could find it a real help to use the words of others. Try dipping into the Psalms in the Bible and reading some of these slowly to God. Many of them are prayers that have been used by others for generation after generation.

We can share even our deepest feelings with God—after all, he knows them anyway. And you're never going to catch him by surprise. He won't respond, "I never knew that!"

At the same time, talking with God is not meant to be like him listening to a podcast—all one way. God wants to share his thoughts and feelings back to us too.

Sure, God is ever ready to listen to the words on our lips and the unspoken feelings of our heart. But he'd also like us to give him the space to prompt our spirit and touch our mind. Which means if you do run out of things to say it might be a good thing as then you might get around to listening.

Getting kick-started. Perhaps you are thinking, "But where do I start?" Forgive me, but I am going to have to go back to the baby nursery for just a moment. The simple answer is, "Start with a few coos and dribbles."

That Father and child relationship we've been talking about is not like the ones in those black and white films of yesteryear—where sons called their father "sir" and hugged them as often as they would a bank manager. That's not what Jesus had in mind, as we can know from his own language.

The first dribbling word a Jewish baby may utter is *"Abba"*—which roughly translates as "Dada." And that's exactly the word we hear Jesus using as he prays when preparing to die on the cross.[93] There's nothing posh or formal here and there need not be for us, either.

Come to that, what makes you think God's fussed about hearing a long eloquent speech from you anyway? Have you ever been present when some infant burbled its first word—no matter how incomprehensible it actually was?

Remember the shrieks of joy and ecstasy that broke out—even though it was probably nothing more than a burp? Take it from me, God will be equally happy over your first infant mumblings.

Food For Thought

Back to plants and another thing they need—food. Whether you think in terms of rain or fertilizer the principle is the same—strong plants get that way through nourishment.

Of course, prayer is part of that process. But the mainstay of our spiritual nourishment is God's written word—the Bible. You want to know God better, to see how he acts, to know what excites him, makes him mad, and what he does about it? Well, God's put it all in writing for you.

The Bible is not just some tired old historical tome written centuries ago by irrelevant people. The Bible is actually "alive." In fact, the Bible describes itself as "living and active. Sharper than any double-edged sword, it penetrates even to dividing soul and spirit, joints and marrow; it judges the thoughts and attitudes of the heart."[94] And you thought it was just a big old book?

The Bible is God's message to you and the world. It is how he gives us the wisdom to live in ways that are best for us and others. And the way for us to fill our minds with all that is true about him; to discover the details of his character, plans, and purposes.

No wonder the Bible continues to outsell every other book worldwide every week. But how can you make the most of it? Here are a few suggestions.

Read chunks at a time. The Bible was written to be consumed banquet-style, not snacked on like calorie-counting nibbles. So try to read it that way. Take whole sections and read them at one go.

In this way, it's like drinking a whole barrel of wholesome fertilizer—it fills you, feeds you, and helps you keep on growing. It's good always to be looking out for what it shows you about God and how he feels and acts toward us. And don't rush. Sometimes press your "pause button" and stay with a story or a picture to allow what you read to kindle your imagination as well as enlighten your mind.

Whatever you do, don't aim to start at the beginning and read through to the end. Because somewhere at about page 124 or so you are going to get horribly stuck. And that's because the Bible is not one big book like *War and Peace*. It's a collection of books that are there for different reasons.

So start with something like the stories of Jesus' life, which are found in the first four books of the New Testament. And get your hands on a modern translation that's easy to read, such as the *Contemporary English Version* or *Good News Bible*.

Read with a willingness to discover and act. As you read, ask yourself "Why was this written down?" "What did it have to say to those who first read it?" and "How does it apply to me, my family, my work, and my friends?"

And ask God to show you the answers to those questions. Look for him to nudge you as you read. Notice where it makes you go "wow." And where you go "ouch." And figure out what you should do about it.

What about the bits you don't understand? Park them for later. The real issue is the things you do understand. Make sure they become part of your life.

At times the Bible will be food for your soul. At other times it will be the gardener's pruning shears. Both are essential for healthy growth.

Memorize some of it. When you come to something in the Bible that particularly strikes you, find a way to lock it into your memory. Jot it down and stick it by your mirror, turn it into a computer screen saver, program it into your cell phone display. Do anything that will help you let it fill your mind and help you to chew on it.

One reason for doing this may be to reinforce something God wants you to be sure you have grasped and made your own. Let's say you have a certain fear—like that of facing a new challenge at work—you might want to memorize something that expresses the way God will always be there for you.

Read it with others. Don't get too "driven" about spending hours reading the Bible by yourself—particularly if reading is not something you do much anyway. It's only been for the past two hundred years or so that the followers of Jesus have been able to carry the Bible with them anyhow.

What will make a difference is to dig into the Bible with two or three other people—or more. Take it in turns to look for "wows" and "ouches." Share what you discover together. And do it often.

Be Ready to Pollinate

The reason there are so many flowers is all down to pollination. The breeze blows, pollen spreads, and new life begins. The good news about Jesus—which you have experienced for yourself—spreads in the same kind of way. And produces the same kind of results.

The breeze of God's Spirit blows, what we know about Jesus makes a journey to someone else and, sometimes, it takes root and grows.

You are part of that process. It's nothing to lose sleep over or break into a sweat about. It's part of normal life.

But remember two things.

Don't get up people's noses. You know what happens when pollen gets up nostrils. So don't do it. Be a fragrance, not an irritant when it comes to sharing what you have discovered about Jesus.

You don't have to dump pollen all over people who don't want it. But you'll notice that the more attractive the flower of your life grows, the more people will want to have a sniff.

Choose your moment. There is a season when pollen is most likely to "take." It's the season when the other plant is ready for it. In the same way, there will be the times when people want to hear. And these are the best moments to explain what has become real to you.

Remember, just like pollination in nature, God is part of the process. He's the one who prepares people for what they hear and helps you say what needs to be said. Part of the good news to us is the final promise Jesus made to the disciples—his pollinators. He promised, "I will be with you always, even until the end of the world."[95] And that includes you.

Join a Fragrant Bunch

Plants don't exist by themselves. They are part of an intricate ecological system. The same is true of those who follow Jesus. Our faith may be personal but it's not solitary.

Being part of a group who are traveling in the same direction as you is not an option. It's an absolute essential. We need others for our spiritual survival and have a part to play in theirs.

There's strength in numbers. Take a stick and bend it and it will quickly snap in half. Take 10 or 20, place them together like one thick branch, and it would take a chainsaw to do the same job.

The same is true for us. If we try to make a go of our relationship with Jesus on our own, we are vulnerable to the pressure that can snap our faith in two. But there is strength in numbers. So use it.

We need others to encourage us down the path of life and to help hold us up when things get tough, confusing, and even discouraging. Just like Dorothy had Toto, the Scarecrow, Tin-man, and the Lion—so we, too, have one another to journey with down life's yellow brick and mud-spattered road.

And we will arrive at the desired destination one day—but we will only do it together.

The Big Picture

What I've spoken about so far is the importance of you being part of a small group of like-minded people—like Dorothy and chums. But the picture is far bigger than that. As a follower of Jesus you are into something vast. Let me try to give you the panoramic perspective.

Are you familiar with the children's television phenomenon called *Power Rangers*? In this Japanese-style kick-fest, five Californian kids use their karate-chop powers to protect the planet. Much fun is had by the fabulous five while they prance and pummel themselves in true Bruce Lee fashion—while wearing colored leotards no respectable planet-saver would be seen dead in.

The thing is, when fighting individually, it's soon clear they couldn't beat their way out of a children's birthday party. They get pulverized by the nifty nasties invading their world.

But watch out. Because when these kids get in trouble they fit together to make one huge great mechanical monster so scary that even the great Godzilla would soil himself at the sight of it.

These five punchers are useless on their own—but by becoming united there is no stopping them. And this is what has happened to those of us who are followers of Jesus. We have become one. We are called the Church—which isn't a building or a program of activities—but a united body primed for action.

Like the Power Rangers, by ourselves we are beaten. But together we can be all that God intends. Even without the colored leotards.

One of the first Christian leaders, the apostle Paul, used an image a little closer to home than these Jurassic juveniles. He called the Church the Body of Christ.[96] He wanted us to see ourselves as the limbs or organs that all belong to one another—each with a different role to play but essential to the others.

The Global Garden

This is all far bigger than you can ever imagine. To think in gardening terms again it is a vast plantation stretching from horizon to horizon and beyond. And that is only a part of it.

The garden of history. The Church is the only organization that never loses a member through death. But don't think in terms of the believers of old now being some decaying compost heap in the sky. They are celebrating with the whole population of heaven and are just as alive as we are. In fact, even more so.

They include young and old, rich and poor, unknown and mega-famous. Heaven is full of history-makers, life-changers, and unknown and seemingly insignificant people too . . . and those whose shadow we are not worthy to shelter under. They are all our people. Trillions of them. We are part of that magnificent Body and they are part of us.

The garden of geography. Worldwide there is a vast multitude of different expressions of the Body of Jesus.

In Latin America it takes stadium-sized buildings to cater for congregations—with as many as 80,000 meeting to worship and learn together. In other countries that it would be best not to name they meet secretly in homes, a few at a time, due to persecution.

Elsewhere the Body meets in hotels, public halls, schools, church buildings, the open air, gymnasiums, cathedrals, and under bamboo roofs.

Some worship in silence, others to a Latin beat, others with the fervor of rock 'n' roll—and seemingly everything and anything in between. Some use written prayers, some seem to busk it, while others use a laptop and LCD projector. Some even use lasers and dry ice.

Every major culture is represented in the worldwide Church. The Body of Jesus is as varied as the flora in London's Kew Gardens.

This vast company of people all have one thing in common—they worship Jesus as Lord of their lives and have come to know God as a personal friend and Father. Day by day, week by week, they celebrate their new life with Jesus. And you're a part of it. This is the vast garden in which you have been planted.

The Reason For the Garden

Gardens and bodies exist for a purpose. They are not there just to "be" but also to "do." So far as the Body of Jesus is concerned, we exist to do what he did. Literally "to be his body"—together bringing and being good news wherever we are and whenever we can.

There have been times when the Church has failed miserably in that role. But there have been others when the compassion of Jesus shown through the actions of his Body on Earth has transformed relationships, families, communities, and even nations.

Hospitals, the hospice movement, and the drive to bring education to the masses all had their roots in the Body of Jesus at work. So did the end of the slave trade, social reforms to protect children, women, and the disadvantaged, the fight to end global poverty—and much more.

We are to be salt

Jesus said his followers were to have the same impact as salt.[97] And when they heard him they knew exactly what he meant. Salt was what they used to preserve meat. Just like salt, Jesus wants to use us like a preservative—holding back the growth of evil and decay, acting like a purifying agent to make things cleaner.

In Jesus' day, salt was also a cleansing and healing agent. And as salt we are to bring healing to wounded and hurting people.

We are to be a light set on a hill

Jesus also told his followers they were to be like the lights of a city.[98] And they knew what that meant too. In a world without streetlights the traveler would see the collection of lights from houses on a hill and know they were heading in the right direction. Those who follow Jesus are to live lives that help people find the way.

This does not involve making a claim to be superior or more important than anyone else. It just means we are to be a living example of the way life is intended to be—and so help others find the way for themselves.

What's It All For Anyway?

Ultimately what is it that should motivate us to live as God intends? In the end, there is only one thing—our response to Jesus because of who he is and all he has done for us.

There's a somewhat strange concept toward the end of the Bible that expresses perfectly why we follow Jesus. It's a description of what happens when time comes to an end. As the end captions of history roll, we are told heaven will be like a great wedding feast—a celebration to end all celebrations.

But there's more. The wedding is between Jesus "the bridegroom" and his Church—us the bride.[99]

To a man like me the thought of being a "bride" sounds rather scary. But there is something behind the concept that's very revealing and worth getting our heads around. And to do so we need to understand the wedding customs of Jesus' time.

When a girl became promised in marriage she was given the cloth to make her own wedding dress. And she went diligently and lovingly to work. In her mind was that moment when she and the one she loved would meet face to face.

Hour upon hour she would labor. Every stitch, tuck, and piece of intricate embroidery demonstrated the love she had for her future husband. There was no other motivation behind all she did.

I have seen something very much like this firsthand. From the vantage point of being the groom's father I watched my son's bride arrive alongside him. She had devoted hours of detailed planning and preparation into this one moment. And the message was written all over her radiant face—"I did this all for you because I love you."

It's the same with all we do. It's not just that we want to live cleaner, more worthwhile lives. Or to make our street, neighborhood, workplace, and world a better place to be. Or that we need to make ourselves useful until the time comes. It's because each act—wherever we are and whatever we are doing—contributes to our wedding outfit—that thing which displays our love for Jesus.

One day we will meet Jesus face to face. His body will carry the marks of his love. And we will be wearing the evidence of ours. There can be no better reason for serving him than that he is worth it. And, as millions have already discovered, he is. Which is what I hope you are now in the process of discovering too.

So that's it. You've made it to the end. Unless you cheated and have just started here. But let's assume you've played it straight. That the ton of elephant dung, the shopping cart with the bent wheel, the tin squash ball, and the giant boulders blocking the road are now all behind you. That's history. But what's more important is what is ahead of you. My hope—and prayer—is that it's a life of adventure and fulfillment in following Jesus. Because there is nothing better.

NOTES

Finding Your Way Through the References

This book claims Jesus said and did certain things. You need to know we're not making it up—and to read it for yourself if you wish. So we've shown you where to look in the record of his life that's included in the Bible.

For example, to find Luke 3:22, use the table of contents in the front of a Bible to find the "book" of Luke. The number "3" shows the chapter of Luke, while "22" refers to the verse within that chapter.

Chapter 2
[1] Genesis 1:1

Chapter 4
[2] John 20:28,29
[3] John 14:9
[4] John 10:30
[5] Matthew 10:40
[6] John 8:58
[7] Luke 5:17–26
[8] See Mark 14:61,62
[9] John 8:32

Chapter 5
[10] See Mark 15:34

Chapter 6
[11] See John 19:32
[12] See John 19:34
[13] John 19:38-40
[14] John 20:15,16
[15] John 20:3-8
[16] See John 20:19
[17] Luke 24:13-35
[18] John 20:25-29
[19] John 21:4-13
[20] 1 Corinthians 15:6

Chapter 7
[21] See John 10:10
[22] See Matthew 23:23-33
[23] Isaiah 53:6
[24] Isaiah 59:2

Chapter 8
[25] Luke 23:4
[26] Mark 10:33,34
[27] See John 12:32
[28] See Matthew 20:28
[29] See John 10:18
[30] Matthew 26:53
[31] Matthew 27:30
[32] Matthew 27:12-14
[33] Matthew 27:50
[34] Micah 5:2
[35] Isaiah 7:14
[36] Psalm 41:9
[37] Zechariah 11:12
[38] Isaiah 50:6
[39] Psalm 22:16
[40] Zechariah 12:10
[41] Psalm 22:18
[42] Psalm 34:20
[43] Isaiah 53:9
[44] Psalm 16:10

[45] John 1:29
[46] John 19:30
[47] See Matthew 20:28
[48] See Amos 8:9
[49] Luke 23:44,45
[50] Isaiah 53:5
[51] Matthew 27:46

Chapter 9
[52] John 14:6
[53] See Romans 6:11

Chapter 10
[54] Quoted in Stephen Gaukroger, *It Makes Sense* (Milton Keynes: Scripture Union, 1998)

Chapter 11
[55] Luke 23:43, CEV
[56] See John 14:2
[57] John 14:3, CEV
[58] Matthew 6:19–21
[59] Luke 10:20
[60] Revelation 3:5
[61] Matthew 3:12
[62] Matthew 7:13,14
[63] See John 6:40

Chapter 12
[64] John 3:36
[65] Luke 15:11–32

Chapter 13
[66] Luke 14:25–35
[67] Luke 22:20
[68] Luke 14:27
[69] John 14:15, CEV
[70] Matthew 7:24–27
[71] See Luke 14:33
[72] Luke 14:26

Chapter 14
[73] Romans 8:11
[74] 2 Corinthians 1:22
[75] See Ephesians 3:16
[76] John 3:1–21
[77] John 17:1
[78] Luke 3:22
[79] Matthew 12:31
[80] Matthew 6:9
[81] Mark 14:36
[82] Matthew 7:7–11
[83] See John 10:28
[84] John 16:7
[85] Acts 1:5—note that the word "baptized" could literally be translated "immersed" or "drenched"
[86] John 14:16–18

Chapter 15
[87] See Mark 12:30,31
[88] John 1:12
[89] Mark 14:27–31
[90] Luke 22:54–62
[91] John 21:1–17
[92] 1 John 1:9, CEV

Chapter 16
[93] Mark 14:36
[94] Hebrews 4:12
[95] Matthew 28:20b, CEV
[96] See 1 Corinthians 12:27
[97] Matthew 5:13
[98] Matthew 5:14
[99] Revelation 19:6–9